PLEASE LEAVE QUIETLY

# PLEASE LEAVE QUIETLY
## People, Power & Purpose at Work

Graham Guest

THE SAINT ANDREW PRESS
·EDINBURGH·

First published in 1987 by
THE SAINT ANDREW PRESS
121 George Street, Edinburgh

Copyright © Graham Guest 1987

ISBN 0–7152–0610–9

Illustrations by Richard Boden

**British Library Cataloguing in Publication Data**
Guest, Graham
    Please leave quietly: people, power & purpose at work
    1. Executives——Religious life
    2. Management——Religious aspects——
    Christianity
    I. Title
    248.8'8      BV4596.E93

    ISBN 0–7152–0610–9

Printed in England by St Edmundsbury Press, Bury St Edmunds

# Contents

# Preface

Many people have contributed to the ideas in this text and I am grateful to all of them. Two people deserve special mention—Ian Dillow and the late Donald Hicks. Both of them gave me invaluable encouragement when my will to finish the book was beginning to wilt. Pat Stevens also deserves a special mention for being able to decipher my own rough typing when she was doing such excellent work on the drafts. To all these people, I give my thanks.

*The publisher acknowledges financial assistance from The Drummond Trust towards the publication of this Volume*

# Introduction

'Every morning on my way to work, as I close the front door behind me, I feel as if I am entering an alien world in which Christ is completely unknown and from which he is absent. And when I get back home at night, I feel as if I have returned to a place in which the things he values matter once more'. A manager who works in the City part of London said these words but he was expressing the feeling of many managers. We think of some parts of our world as sacred and others as secular and talk as if God has been squeezed out of the secular part of his world. Of course, there are parts of the world from which God and his rule have been excluded, but he is not absent from our so called secular world on principle. It is just that, since the agricultural societies of the Middle Ages, we have got used to not seeing or looking for him there. A challenge facing Christians today is to allow God to correct our defective eyesight.

This is not a new problem and many people have written about the meaning of the Gospel in our secular society. I lack the skill to add to that literature but I have lived with the problem of our City friend for a long time. I go to church quite regularly and often spend the rest of the week trying to find real, useful connections between what happens in church and what I do in my office. It was from those concerns, starting with real live issues, that this book evolved. As time passed, my thoughts gathered around some of my principal concerns as a manager and, eventually, I selected material which centred around just three of those concerns. These were *leadership*, the use of *power*, and the ways we create the atmosphere of a place in which people work—to use a somewhat fancy word, its *ethos*.

Each individual section of each of the three parts has a common form. An incident from the Bible is used to illustrate a theme which has implications for a manager. A discussion of the incident follows and four or five issues which seem to have been raised are listed. Issues seem to me to be a means to growth and that means thinking and, I would argue, praying. One of my basic beliefs about prayer is that you should pray about the things which you really care about and not those things which various bodies tell you to pray about. God does not need to be reminded of all the causes for concern in this world, but I feel sure that he would like us to take seriously those issues which he has made a real part of our lives. So if there are things about being a manager which concern us deeply, then we should have no alternative but to attempt to work them out with God's help. That process is a part of 'praying the Kingdom' (used in the sense which Charles Elliott uses it in his book *Praying the Kingdom*, Dartman Longman and Todd, London 1985, about ways of praying for political justice and peace and for world economic reform). To help with that process, I have finished each section with a short prayer.

The form of each of these sections is a model which any manager can use simply by taking all of the experience seriously which God has provided at work. We can all develop the sorts of ideas which make up this book and, in the privacy of our own thoughts, it does not matter how well we do it. In a sense, the pieces which make up this book are meditations on management themes. I would not dare to attempt to add to the great literature which exists in that field, but I am interested in helping ordinary managers to connect the things which they do in their workplaces with their basic beliefs about life. That requires quiet thought over a long period. That sort of meditation seems to me to be worth encouraging.

Having said briefly what the book is, I would like to say a word about what it is not. In particular, you will search vainly for any type of erudite theology of industry, commerce, public service or anything else. I do not possess that sort of expertise or knowledge. Equally, there will be many people who have been over this ground many times before and the book may offer them little.

However, there are many ordinary managers who do face real moral and spiritual problems most days of their working life and for whom little help is available. If this book offers them any comfort or strength, my reward is ample. In fact, I would be well satisfied if, as you close the door behind you on the way to work tomorrow morning, you reflected, just for a fleeting second, that you had not left God's world.

# Part I
# The Peter Story

# 1
# People in Organisations

What is the most important resource which a manager uses on behalf of an organisation? Apart from the most exceptional cases, the answer must be its people. 'Man-management' is a phrase which can be found in somewhat old-fashioned management text books. Even before the growth in the popularity of that phrase, considerable emphasis was given to developing team spirit, often at schools out on the playing fields. If we look through any modern management text book, people figure high in the lists of subjects which are covered. Elton Mayo thought about matching jobs to the levels of the capabilities of individual people. Elliott Jacques worked on the place of people in organisations and phenomena like spans of control. Chris Argyris took the needs of men in organisations as one of his subjects. Frederick Hertzberg investigated motivation. Rensis Likert's research concerned responsibility and other topics, and so on—the list is endless. Over a long period there has been a growing concern for the part people play in our industrial society.

People in society are God's concern. Industry, commerce and the public services are important parts of our modern world and God is concerned about the people who work in those aspects of our society. Mayo and all the other management researchers have given us important insights into people's behaviour in these social areas. Despite their efforts and although many people have written at length about being a Christian citizen in modern times, there is no widely accepted, coherent view of how God relates to the people in our world of work. However we do have the Bible and it is full of people who sought after and found God in their everyday life. One way of understanding God's relationship to our world of work is to use the stories of those lives to discover parts of the relationship. One such life belonged to Peter.

At the start of his ministry, Jesus recruited Peter into his team. Peter became a saint eventually. His career development was so startling that any manager would have been proud to have had a hand in it. It forms a case history and it gives us insights into how we might develop our own man–management style.

# 2 A New Follower

*'Follow me and I will make you fishers of men'* (Matthew 4:19).

In three short years, Jesus selected his men, trained them and sent them out to the greatest mission mankind has ever known. As a project, it dwarfs the Apollo space programme or any other that man has launched. Within a few years of Jesus' death, his men were taking the Gospel to the four corners of the earth. In Acts we are told that the learned men of the day thought of Peter as a poor, ignorant fisherman and it seems likely that his broad Galilean accent would classify him as a country yokel as far as they were concerned. Yet, Jesus picked him. In doing so, Jesus showed more insight into human potential than most of our modern staff selection techniques allow us to show. Jesus picked a winner.

There are three important things about this recruitment story: Jesus had a reputation, he knew what he was doing, and he told Peter and Andrew what they would be doing in language they could understand.

Peter and his brother Andrew joined Jesus. We do not know, but it is a fair supposition that they knew a great deal about Jesus already. Since they were fishermen down by the water, they must have known about the mission of John the Baptist. People must have talked about the baptism of Jesus, and John had probably told his followers about Jesus. We know that John advised his own followers to join Jesus and it is likely that the reputation of Jesus was spreading and that it had reached Peter and Andrew. Our workplaces have reputations which influence people when they think of joining us. If the secular world really is God's world, and if people are joining us to do their part of God's work, what sort of reputation should we have? What is our local reputation like? Is our workplace regarded as a good place to work and how would God have us define a 'good place'. What should a university appointments board be saying about us? Some managers, particularly specialists, have reputations which attract people. They might be well-known exciting research workers for example. They might have a good training reputation. Whatever it is, Jesus wants it to be a Godly reputation and we all have a duty to fashion it accordingly. If we do not have a reputation for being a good employer, we should not be in the recruitment business.

In his own mind, Jesus knew what his business was. As a boy he went about his Father's business. As a man, he preached the Kingdom of God, the Kingship of his Father. We need to know what our business is and what part in it we shall ask the recruit to play. It is immoral for us to recruit people into positions which have not been worked through carefully. For a new graduate to get his/her first experience of incompetent handling leading to frustration, anger and despondency at our hands is a sin which ought to be avoided. If we do not know what we are asking a new recruit to do, we should not be in the recruitment business.

Apart from having a reputation and knowing what his job in life was and what Peter's would be, Jesus explained that task in simple language. If you ever read a job description given to a new employee, look at it from that new employee's point of view. Most of it will be couched in such general terms that it could mean anything that the Company chooses. Some job descriptions contain an escape clause which allows management to slip in anything they please. It is probable that any substantive clause requires the use of a Company jargon dictionary before any meaning can be gathered from it. Jesus said to two simple fishermen, 'I will make you fishers of men,' and they followed him to the ends of the earth. If we are not able to tell people meaningfully what we want them to do for us, we should not be in the recruitment business.

Jesus spent three years with his disciples. They saw him preach. He taught them how to pray. He took them on retreats. He sent them out two by two on a training tour of duty. His training was practical. For instance, when they went on their training tour, he told them not to waste time at a place if things were not going well —excellent advice if you are building up someone's confidence. When Jesus invited Simon and Andrew to join him, he must have worked out the main features of the next few years for them. If we do not know how we are going to help people to develop and move towards the maturity God has planned for them, we should not be in the recruitment business.

If we recruit someone and ask them to work for us for eight hours a day, we are accepting a considerable responsibility for one of God's children. If we have not thought that through, we should not be in the recruitment business.

## Things to think about

1   Do we have a systematic way of examining each job we ad-
    vertise to make sure that, in God's eyes, it is a job worth doing?
2   Think of the last job we filled. In what ways could we have
    improved the preparation for the interview, the explanation of
    the job to the candidate and his introduction to the work?
3   In our last interview, what sort of judgments were we making?
    Would God have been satisfied with those judgments?
4   Put down on a sheet of paper the process we use to recruit
    people. As a process, could we defend it before God? What
    should be done to improve it?

## Prayer

Lord Jesus, in your earthly life you chose people to work for
you and gave them fulfilment in that work. May we prepare
carefully each time we try to recruit someone to work for us. Give
us the ability to explain clearly to that person what his future
work will be. If he joins us, help us to prepare effectively for his
coming. In all these actions, make your will for him our prime
consideration.

*Amen*

# 3  A Job Worth Doing

*'I will make you fishers of men'* (Matthew 4:19).

Jesus had a job which he wanted Peter to do for him and he used
Peter's own experience to tell him what that job would be. Our
image of a fisherman's job is probably a lot less rich than Peter's
must have been and as a result we lose most of the message which
Jesus gave to Peter. Perhaps we do get beyond the image of a
comfortable spot for fly fishing in the Scottish Highlands on a lazy
summer's afternoon. But we probably do not get far beyond the
picture of each man getting hooked safely and being brought
into the boat which is the Church—or some such idea. For sure,
such images are nowhere near any which might have existed in
the minds of Andrew and Peter when Jesus gave them this job
description.

   Making a living from a little boat on the Sea of Galilee was no
easy matter. On that sea, very peculiar storms do blow up quickly

because of the hills which surround it. One such perilous storm is recorded in the Gospels. We know that it was possible to toil all night and have nothing to show for it. If we sit down and think for a while, we know that our own deep sea fishermen with all their modern radar and other gadgets do not have an easy time. Deep sea fishing is one of the most dangerous modern industries. But there is another side to the picture as well. When Jesus told his disciples to drop the net over the side of the boat, they brought in a huge catch. It is almost certain that Peter and Andrew knew the joys of a good day's fishing out on the Sea of Galilee in fine weather and they knew what it meant to their families to bring home a really good catch which was going to set the family budget right for some time. When Jesus asked Peter and Andrew to come and fish for men, the image in their minds must have been rich, a real man's job, full of challenge, full of possibilities for work, job satisfaction, surprise, disappointment and all sorts of other things which made it a job worth doing.

The Bible says that men are to grow to the fullness of the stature of Christ. Professor William Barclay, in one of his books, tells of an epitaph on a tombstone in Scotland which says, 'He was born a man and died a grocer'. There is nothing wrong with any job which makes a man more of a man, including being a grocer. There is a great deal wrong with a job which does not allow and cause a man to grow, or worse still, causes him to become stunted and die spiritually. When Jesus offered Peter the job as a fisher of men, he must have been fully aware of the challenges which were going to come Peter's way. The route from being a simple Galilean fisherman to a cross in Rome was a growth route for Peter. When Peter hung on that cross in Rome, he must have been as near to the fullness of the stature of Christ as any man has ever been.

I have watched many new graduates join the research departments in which I have worked. In the first two years, it is important for them to get well-defined, purposeful jobs that they can do and in which they can be successful. As they accept more responsibility in their mid-twenties, the management problems with which they are left to cope should be reasonably easy to solve. Their basic attitudes to work should be vigorous and healthy, not ones born of disillusion. As they mature, through their thirties, they need to become thoughtful, mature people, capable of introducing order into other people's tangled thought processes. When they are mature, they should be able to guide projects through political and intellectual storms. Some such development process lies in front of each new person we recruit and we should have that in mind when we recruit them.

Our responsibility as managers for the growing stature of every person placed by God in our care is as clear as a bell. That responsibility does not start when, in the midst of a crisis, we put in some ill-considered and mal-administered staff development scheme in order to try to sort out a few of the mid-life casualties which we have helped to create. That responsibility starts months before we recruit any single person. We must make sure that every job which we offer represents in some sense or other an opportunity for that person to serve and to grow.

When Jesus invited Peter to become a fisher of men, the job was not a spot of quiet fly fishing on a lazy river on a warm summer's afternoon. It was an invitation to sail to Rome through storms and winds such as Peter knew on the Sea of Galilee and to become a saint. The jobs we offer to others should have similar characteristics.

## Things to think about

1   How much thought do we give to the stature development potential of the jobs which we offer to people?
2   Think about the last person we recruited. What sort of a job was on offer and how much thought have we given to that new employee's subsequent development?
3   Jesus recruited Peter by referring to his rich experience in his present job. Have we recruited people from rich rewarding jobs in other organisations? Is our latest such recruit of that type a fulfilled or a bitterly disillusioned man?
4   It is not easy to construct suitably challenging jobs and to keep them that way. What can we do about the way things are done at our workplace to make that more possible?

## Prayer

Lord Jesus, when you recruited Peter and Andrew, you set before them the challenging possibility of becoming fishers of men. When we recruit people, may we have in mind jobs which allow people to grow towards the goal which you have set for each one of them. May those jobs be challenges for them and a source of joy and fulfilment.

*Amen*

# 4 Starting to Serve

*'Getting into one of the boats which was Simon's, Jesus asked him to push out a little from the land and he sat down and taught the people'* (Luke 5:3).

Jesus was preaching. We do not know why he asked Peter to take his boat a little way from the shore for him. Maybe the shoreline was difficult in some way. Maybe the crowd was pushing in on him. We do not know. We do know that Peter had a boat nearby and he used it to enable Jesus to sit down and preach to the people in a lot more comfort. We also know that, after the work was done, Jesus told Peter to let down his nets and that in doing so he caught a great many fish. That catch must have been one of the most memorable for Peter. In later life, it must have provided him with one of his best fisherman's stories—the ones that did not get away.

Jesus wanted to do a job, to preach the Gospel to that crowd and he had a problem. He needed a place from which to preach. He could have asked Peter to do a quite impossible job like moving the crowd back. But he did not do that. Peter had a boat and could use it, so Jesus took Peter's possessions and abilities and used them. Peter must have felt needed and wanted and useful. At the beginning of his career path, Peter saw his gifts and his talents used. It was a pattern that he was going to see repeated throughout his life.

Peter must have missed a day's fishing to help Jesus. It had cost Peter his time and the job had used his skill. It may have been quite tricky to keep that boat steady for an hour or two and it would certainly have demanded his attention. For that service, Peter was thanked properly. The Bible pictures God as a Father whose generosity knows no bounds. Perhaps one should not lay too much or the wrong sort of emphasis on it, but the fact is that, after an afternoon's service, God's generosity made up for everything that Peter might have lost by his service. The story seems to suggest that there was a huge bonus as well, and Jesus was concerned that Peter should lose nothing.

When an experienced person leaves and we have to recruit and train a new person, it is very easy to compare the two very much to the disadvantage of the newcomer. It is sad to see a manager harking back to the 'better' former days when their old friends were around 'to put some zip into things'. It is tragic when, in pursuit of memories and old times, a manager fails to see the potential that he/she has in the new employee. It is our job to look for potential and gifts which people *do* have and to use them carefully and wisely. Above all, we should not spend our time grumbling about qualities we think they *ought* to have.

Given a little careful searching, a manager can find people with research skills. Even if your product is ideas, you can find other people who can sell them for you. It is difficult to find both of these skills in one person. I had been particularly fortunate and had had such a person for several years. He left and I missed him. It took me at least a year to realise that I was seriously undervaluing his replacement, secretly and unconsciously resenting having to compensate for the changed skills available to me and generally behaving without true wisdom, generosity and courtesy.

Of course, I had all sorts of excuses—work pressed on all sides, changing my behaviour was an inconvenience. I saw none of these things. I did not even see that the replacement was a better man in many ways than the one who had left.

'Thank you' is a word which we should use frequently and practise diligently. Frequently it is the only immediate recognition of service which is available to us. Due to my own stupidity, I overlooked many of the thank-yous which I ought to have said to my new research man. I should have seen and acknowledged more generously the work which he was doing.

If we look at the career development of Peter, it is thrilling. After three years with Jesus, he became the first person to preach the Gospel in Acts. He was the person behind the mission to the Jews. His stories and experiences went into Mark's Gospel and he wrote letters which found their way into the New Testament. That career was started by Jesus recognising and using his gifts as a fisherman. Judging by his determination to follow that path, Peter must have felt it well worth while and amply rewarding.

As managers we need to see, use and develop the natural gifts which our people possess and we need to say thank you.

## Things to think about

1   Is it part of our basic management philosophy to use other people's skills and abilities? Or do we get bogged down thinking about the things they ought to be able to do?
2   Think of our number one staff failure. Have we looked at that person's abilities sufficiently carefully and tried hard to use them?
3   What part do thanks and acknowledgment of service play in our lives? How should we improve our performance?

4 Think about one of our basic management processes—say progress meetings. What place do thanks and being appreciative have in those systems?

## Prayer

Lord Jesus, you took the gifts which Peter possessed, used them in your service and rewarded him abundantly. Teach us to look for, to use and to appreciate the gifts and talents of those who are around us. May we never hanker after those gifts which they do not have. May our use of their gifts cause them to grow in your service and in the service of their fellow men.

*Amen*

# 5 The Impulsive Follower

*'Jesus immediately reached out his hand and caught him, saying to him, "O man of little faith, why did you doubt?"'* (Matthew 14:31).

After having spent some time with the disciples, Jesus wanted to be alone and so the disciples had crossed the lake by themselves. The crossing had been rough and this particular verse comes towards the end of the episode. Peter had jumped into the water before the boat had reached the shore, presumably in order to get to Jesus more quickly. Despite the fact that he was an experienced fisherman, he got into trouble, called out desperately for help and it appears that Jesus grabbed hold of him and pulled him to the shore and safety. Peter was at his impulsive best. There are other examples of Peter's impulsive behaviour in the Gospels, and he comes through them all, often because Jesus acts to make that the case.

Jesus never encouraged his followers to be impulsive and to act without thought. The reverse is true. His stories are full of cautionary tales about unwise maidens and their lamps, watchful servants and people who count the cost before starting to build. He tells the disciples to beware false prophets and to prepare to take up their cross. It is true that Jesus chastises Peter for his lack of faith rather than anything else in this particular case but that cannot be used to justify impulsive action. Fundamentally, in as far as they are able, Jesus expects people to make adequate preparation for their work for him.

Peter had one big thing in his favour in this incident. Maybe his faith did crack a little and maybe a fisherman like himself ought to have had more sense than to get into trouble in the water, but his heart was in the right place and he was striking out in the direction of Jesus. Jesus did rap his knuckles just a little, but he also grabbed hold of him firmly and pulled him in towards the shore.

Impulsiveness in a person who is trying hard to do the right thing is a very forgivable weakness. If we have ever struggled to get all the pieces in the right places in some management jigsaw, we know the temptation to be impulsive only too well. That complex plan for instance, when we are going to spend months 'dotting all the i's and crossing all the t's'—why not let it roll? There are times when we have to rush into a situation, make a few quick decisions about how to tackle the problems and get on with it. At other times a few quick, impulsive actions can get rid of a lot of frustrations. There is a Peter lurking in each one of us, ready to jump out of the boat and to strike out towards the shore as best we can.

Changing organisations was a major part of my work. After persuading the various parties involved in the change to go down a particular road, there always came a point when I had to write it all down carefully and get it all finally agreed. I had to put myself into other people's shoes and see that document through their eyes. I was always amazed by the interpretations which were put on simple phrases. Very rarely, I just could not be patient and I would make a document available long before it was ready. I always paid heavily for my impulsiveness and found myself in deep water. Sometimes, my own people did the same thing and I found myself trying desperately to extract them from their troubles.

The other side of the coin is just as bad, if not worse. Jesus is just as much against people being over-anxious as he is against them being impulsive. The boat does not have to be rammed hard against the shore and stuck in the sand before we dare contemplate putting our toe, somewhat gingerly, onto firm ground. That is taking excessive thought for the day and the evils thereof. As managers, we should take reasonable risks rather than wait all the time for absolute certainties.

Impulsiveness is not the only, or the most important, topic in this passage, especially for a manager. Maybe Jesus did give Peter a sharp verbal clip round the ears, but he also pulled him out of the water. Our prime responsibility to our own people is to see that they get to the shore safe and sound, and we should never have any doubts about that. This is especially the case if they are trying to do something for us personally or to get alongside us in some situation. After the episode has finished, maybe for their own good, we ought to point out to them that, with a little more care, they could have avoided the problem. Our power, experience and standing in the organisation have been given to us so that we might serve them, especially in times of their need. Those times of need include escapades, like Peter's, in which they should have been more sensible.

## Things to think about

1   How do we draw the line between foolish impulsiveness and trusting faith in God or another person?
2   When was the last time that we acted impulsively and when was the last time that a little more faith and impulsiveness might not have been misplaced?
3   What was the last impulsive action by one of our people which caused us problems? What was our reaction?
4   It takes coolness, strength and other qualities to extract people from the consequences of their own foolishness. Do we have these qualities or should we develop them?

## Prayer

Lord Jesus, when Peter came to you in his joy and excitement through the water, you saved him from the difficulties into which he had fallen through his own impulsiveness. Teach us to have due care when we act and to learn to help others when they act foolishly. May we learn to keep the right balance between lacking due care and being over-anxious, so that we can serve you to the best of our ability in all things.

*Amen*

## 6 Fundamental Commitment

*'You are the Christ'* (Mark 8:29).

'You are the Christ'. These must be Peter's most famous words and rightly so. The Messiah, the King like David, the one who was going to restore Israel to her former glory, the one who was going to bring the chosen nation to greatness—these were the ideas which made the blood of a true Israelite race through his body. At the time of Christ, Israel was in a ferment based on these Messianic ideas. Bands of freedom fighters—the Zealots—wandered abroad, just like those which existed in Africa in the last days of the European Empires. It was only a few years later that Rome decided enough was enough as far as Israel was concerned. The Romans marched into Jerusalem and sacked and destroyed the temple and much of the city. Such was the power and the effects of the Messianic idea.

If the Israelites had listened to their own prophets, they would have found that there was another image of the Messiah as well as that of another David or Maccabees. The suffering servant and the lamb of God images were the ones which Jesus adopted and they were the ones about which Peter would learn. He was going to leave everything and follow Jesus as that other type of Messiah. However, at this point in time, all Peter knew was that Jesus was the Messiah and thus his commitment was complete.

There has always been two types of belief or commitment in the world. In ancient times, they were typified by the Jewish and the Greek interpretations of what was important about a be-lief. A Greek was concerned that something was 'academically' true—for example, that the medicine on the shelf would cure the disease. The Jew believed in the medicine and he drank it. For the Greek, his central concern, his God, was a collection of rather abstract qualities. For the Jew, God was the God who led Israel out of the land of Egypt, and there was nothing abstract about that. When Peter came to believe in Jesus as Messiah, he was not taking up some abstract philosophical position—he was well on his way to a personal faith in Jesus which acknowledged the power of Jesus to lead the new Israel into and within the re-established Kingdom of God.

Most Christians would argue that their faith is faith in a person, Jesus Christ. That must be true in the ultimate. But that faith causes people to value those things which he stood for and to act on them. As St John says, for example, 'He who does not love his brother, whom he has seen, cannot love God whom he has not seen' (1 John 4:20). Our faith is our ultimate concern. Our ultimate concern, that for which we will give everything, is our faith.

It is this sort of faith and total commitment that determines the ultimate nature of a man's life. Managers can have that sort of faith and commitment to a variety of things—power and money being two of the most common. We all know people who are as cunning as they come, sticking to just the right side of the law and the company rule book and, in the process, acquiring immense power.

Such people have put their faith in their own gods and they will follow their own messiahs to their sort of promised land.

In my latter years as a manager I had comparatively little to do with our new graduate intake each year, but I felt, and still feel very strongly that, during their first two years, they should experience well directed work patterns which show to them how rich and rewarding work can be. On one occasion, I was horrified to discover a new recruit being bounced from pillar to post by an administrative system which had gone awry. Whether my colleagues liked it or not, I plucked the girl out of that mess and, whether or not it was an appropriate use of my time, I personally made quite sure that her work and her training became more purposeful. I do not know whether this was good management. I do know that the appropriate treatment of young recruits was one of my ultimate concerns.

Most people have some set of fundamental beliefs for which they will die, spiritually if not factually. Managers have them. We need research directors for whom scientific truth commands their total commitment. We need finance directors committed to honesty, personnel directors committed to people, and everyone committed to those aspects of godliness which are at the centre of their job. When Peter recognised explicitly that Jesus was the Messiah, he had taken his fundamental commitment an important step forward by verbalising and crystalising it into understandable, usable words. Many people would argue that our beliefs and way of life is limited by not being made explicit and verbalised. If we think that the things of God are the most important things at the centre of our worklife, then we need to verbalise that commitment and say what it means in real hard terms.

During his life, Peter made a lot of mistakes—you can read about them in the New Testament. But once he had said, 'You are the Christ', there was never any doubt about who was at the centre of his life. We need to know who and what are at the centre of our lives. If we spend eight hours a day being a manager, then some of those ultimate concerns ought to be about the nature of management.

## Things to think about

1   Is it true that our fundamental beliefs have determined the nature of the lives we live? List these beliefs and their effects.
2   When Peter acknowledged Jesus as the Messiah, his commitment to Jesus must have become irresistible. Do we see Jesus in these terms? What else at work do we see in these terms?

3    What management 'gods' do we have around in our lives?
4    Have we thought through and made explicit in our own minds
     the fundamental beliefs that we have about management?

## Prayer

Lord Jesus, we thank you that Peter acknowledged you as Christ
and went out to commit his whole life to your service. Help us to
acknowledge and make explicit your kingship over our lives as
managers and to work out what our service to you should mean
to us.

*Amen*

# 7  Losing the Way

*'Get behind me Satan! For you are not on the side of God, but of men'*
(Mark 8:33).

Earlier in this Gospel story, Peter had seen and had proclaimed that
Jesus was God's Messiah, the Christ. For Peter to have been convinced that this was the case, he must have seen in Jesus everything
that he had ever dreamed about. The teaching of Jesus, the power
he possessed, his ability to answer the learned men of those days—
all of these things added up to being the Messiah in Peter's eyes.
When Jesus started to preach the way of the cross and say that the
cross would be the climax of his own life, Peter must have been
convinced that his ears were deceiving him. How could the
Messiah meet an end like that? In the turmoil of his disbelief, Peter
remonstrated with Jesus and, for his pains, he received this terse
and abrupt answer: J B Phillips translates it, 'You are not seeing
things from God's point of view'.
   By his teaching at that time, and by his death on the cross later,
Jesus was now establishing the central theme of the way of life
which he wanted people to follow. A lifestyle built around the
cross is one which absorbs evil in its various manifestations and
does not pass any part or any derivative of that evil on to someone
else. Christ did that for all of us and he wants us to do that for
others. That way takes many forms. We must turn the other cheek,
and we must return good for evil. Kindness, gentleness, patience,
forbearance, positive charity, wishing the best for others whatever
they wish us, being willing to go the extra mile—all of these
things go to make up the way which we must follow. Ultimately,

we must be willing to suffer for the good of someone else. That is the way of the cross, the way preached and lived out by Jesus. That was what Peter was trying to reject.

The teaching of Jesus about the cross was absolutely clear. His command was, 'Take up your cross and follow me'. Peter learned that and he did it. It may be that the sharp words of Jesus recorded in this passage were etched as indelibly on Peter's mind as the time when he started to learn that lesson. We must learn to follow the same path.

We should be in no doubt that we will meet sin and ungodliness at our place of work. Every time anything falls short of the target in any form whatsoever, there we will see some form of sin. Bad workmanship, poor personnel policies and practices, greed in its many forms including any type of lack of generosity, self-centredness: anything which falls short of positive godliness is sin. There is plenty of it around in our workplace. Jesus is quite emphatic that we can deal with that sin only by going along the way of the cross. If someone is unjust to us, we still give them their rights and treat them as a loving Father would do. If someone does a bad job for us, we must still do our best possible job for him. If someone is rude and overbearing in committees, we must practise courtesy and kindness in return. At work, we must practise the way of the cross all the time.

There is a real danger of debasing the concept of bearing one's cross, especially at work. We often use the phrase to mean tolerating the foolishness of a particular person on a continuing basis. There is something resigned and long-suffering in our debased modern use of that phrase. We know that the chap on that committee is going to sit there for a long time, will continue to introduce long-winded, irrelevant discourses into the discussions and, short of being militantly rude, there is not a thing we can do about it. So he becomes a cross to be borne.

Such a debased concept of cross-bearing has nothing to do with the cross which we should carry. Christ on the cross was God's magnificent act of love and creative redemption. We should hope that men will see their way to repent, *ie* to rethink their action and change. One of the points of being courteous to a discourteous man on a committee is that he might come to value and practise courtesy. We go into a vicious interdepartmental battle and try to settle it in order to bring the creative peace of God to those people. We fight for quality output from people so that they might value quality. It does not matter how tiny a cross we pick up and carry, it is all part of the creative and redemptive work of God in our workplace.

Peter could not see that the way of Christ was the way of the cross. He was off that track, and lost. Just like Peter, we shall get lost on this particular way. Jesus may teach us some sharp lessons, just like Peter. And no matter how often we lose our way, we should remember to get back onto that way as quickly as possible. That is true of work just as much as any other place.

## Things to think about

1   Peter's original concept of the Messiah was weak. Do we have management concepts (such as leadership) which, from God's point of view, are weak?
2   Peter rejected the idea that the cross was going to occupy a central place in Jesus' way of life at first. How central is the cross to our way of life?
3   Think of a major thing which is going wrong at work. Is there a place for a cross somewhere in that situation?
4   What is our reaction to the reply Jesus gave Peter? Are there any sharp lessons around at present which we should be learning?

## Prayer

Lord Jesus, you taught Peter that the cross was central to the way of life in the Kingdom of God. You lived that way out to the full for each of us. You gave us the power to follow that way. Help us never to seek easy solutions that do not work. Help us always to return good for evil and to serve others whatever they do to us.

*Amen*

# 8 Doubts

*'Lo, we have left everything. What shall we have?'* (Matthew 19:27).

Jesus had just been telling the disciples that it was not all that easy to get into the Kingdom of Heaven. Rich men would find it difficult, getting a camel through the eye of a needle would seem a great deal easier to some men. The disciples had just asked Jesus who it was that was going to make the grade when Peter joined in with this remark.

Peter is engagingly human in this episode. He had left everything for Jesus. His sacrifice was, even then, much greater than ours is ever likely to be. Maybe fishing in Galilee was not making Peter into a millionaire, but he was not one of the hired men to whom Jesus referred to in his story either. We would have to be very saintly if the question 'What is there in this for me?' never crossed our minds. At this point in time Peter must have known that he was one of a very tiny band following an unknown rabbi in a remote corner of the Roman Empire. The resurrection and a worldwide Church were in the future, a future completely unknown to Peter. In those circumstances and having just been told about the eye of a needle, what would our reaction have been?

Jesus understood Peter's concern and gave him a reply; not one that criticised him for his lack of faith but one that took him seriously and gave him assurance. First, he made it clear to Peter that, whatever a person does for the Kingdom of God, a generous God will make whatever he needs available to him. He then tells the story of the employer who goes down to the local Job Centre, the marketplace, and employs staff at various times during the day but rewards them all equally generously. It could be that Jesus is telling Peter ever so gently that he had got things the wrong way round. From a worldly point of view, Peter had left a great deal. However, earning our pay and sacrificing are not the sort of relationships we have with God. Basically, Peter had to learn that God provides everything for us to grow in his service.

What do we do with the reaction from our own people—'What is there in this for me?'—especially when it is clear that the road forward is full of difficulties and trouble? One time I carried out a recentralisation of a service. The main case for the move was that small decentralised teams could not maintain the level of expertise required for this work. For a variety of reasons, the year following that reorganisation was bound to be traumatic. Everyone knew that I had been busy painting a picture of the advantages of the new set-up for everyone and I was taken aback by a staff reaction which could be summarised as, 'OK, the future is bright, providing we actually survive the next 12 months, but what's in it for me?' My first reaction was to throw up my hands in horror and start to wonder why I was fighting for a better future for such short-sighted people. Fortunately, I did this in private and had time to think again before I reacted publicly on the issue. Short-term or not, they had a cause for concern which I should have anticipated.

In this world we are surrounded by, and we ourselves are,

gloriously human characters, short-sighted and full of failings, just like Peter. If we do the work which God has set for us and if we do it to his standards, we will be different. We will be in Peter's position and want to ask, 'What is in it for us?' If we try to keep the quality of our work high when we are surrounded by others who get away with murder, we will have our doubts. If we take our people down paths on which a much higher premium is set on basic honesty, consideration for others and similar things, they will react like Peter sometimes. Like Jesus, we must have a reply for them and reassurances to offer them. We must remember that they might feel rather like Peter, as if they are following some rather odd character in one of the more remote departments in our own industrial empire. It would be much easier for them to keep in step with Caesar and everyone else who was behaving 'normally'.

When people do give up a great deal in order to follow us, we have a duty towards those people to reassure and to encourage them. Our reply must reflect the reply which Jesus gave to Peter, namely that any type of Godliness, even just doing things better, carries with it a natural relationship with a generous God which is rewarding beyond our wildest dreams and worth sacrifice. However, we must remember that we have no right to chastise people or reply in anger when they question us about the effects of our leadership on them. They have a right to our considered reply.

## Things to think about

1   Do we know moments of despair and feelings of having lost our direction? How did we react on the last such occasion?
2   How do we feel about rewarding people who have joined us recently, as well as those who have 'toiled with us all day'? This may not have anything to do with money.
3   Is there any sense in which people have made sacrifices for us and for our ideas? How do we recognise this fact in our relationship with them?
4   Peter followed Jesus through this incident and went on to greater things. Have we caused people to lose faith in us and our judgments and to withdraw their commitment? What did we do wrong?

## Prayer

Lord Jesus, you treated Peter very gently when he came to you with his human doubts about having left everything to follow you.

In our work, often we cannot see the purpose of our effort to do work which is of the highest quality, and we have difficulty in explaining to others why they should adopt high standards. Give us the wisdom to think through our reasons and the patience and skill to explain them to other people.

*Amen*

# 9 Not Counting the Cost

*'Lord, I am ready to go with you to prison and to death'* (Luke 22:33).

This part of Luke's Gospel records events which happened towards the end of the ministry of Jesus. The tone of what Jesus was saying changed at this time. The disciples' real service was about to start and the preparation which Jesus was giving to them was orientated towards a more demanding way of life for them. Jesus had just told Peter that things were going to get more difficult for him, that he would be tempted and that he must prepare himself to strengthen others. Impetuous, lovable Peter comes straight back with his comment, 'Lord, I am ready to go with you to prison and to death'.

At no time in the Gospel does Jesus pretend that serving God here on earth is going to be easy. The gate will be narrow. The young man with riches went away sadly. The builder was told to count the cost. The Christian 'way' is the way of the cross and the way of reconciliation—not an easy way at all. In the next part of Luke's Gospel the disciples are sent out on their second mission training exercise, but this time with a big difference. On the first training exercise, they took nothing. This time they had to take whatever they had, including a purse, a bag and a sword. Counting the cost properly and planning were to become much more important in the future but they had not yet learned that. At this moment in time, we see Peter committing himself right up to the hilt without the slightest idea of how to deliver the goods.

As managers, we know just how difficult it is to get a good idea transformed into stable, systematic practice. It does not happen by chance. Enthusiasm may help but that is not all that is required. It is a Godly act to face up to the problems which we may encounter, to count the cost properly and to plan accordingly. Of course, it is true that we cannot plan for everything and we may end up metaphorically 'going to prison' or even 'going to the stake' for our beliefs and actions. When it occurs, such sacrifice has to be for something worthwhile and must be carefully calculated, not the result of some blind, impetuous action.

Jesus accepted Peter's loyal devotion and commitment, but he was very realistic about things. He knew that Peter was going to fall flat on his face and end up by denying him. He knew that Peter was going to learn a lot in a very traumatic way in the next few days. He knew that Peter's faith needed to be built up. He also knew that, in the end, Peter would deliver the goods. The processes by which we learn and by which we teach others to remain enthusiastic, to grow in faith and performance and, in the end, to deliver the goods, are complex. It is a Godly process. It is a process by which people become mature. It is one of the processes by which they grow towards the fullness of the stature of Christ.

We are all too familiar with management situations in which the costs have not been counted properly. My own experience when I was a computer manager some years ago included several examples. I still make excuses and plead special circumstances and there is some truth in all that I say. But the fact is that I did not deliver the goods. In a variety of ways, I caused other people to lose faith, to become disillusioned and, in some cases, to be very greatly inconvenienced. Of course, I did not do it on purpose. My faults were not having the ability or the patience to count the cost properly. Another time I found myself faced by my own computer manager. He was full of anger and resentment about the way I was pushing him. I had some very good organisational and political reasons for wanting him to do something. If I had allowed him to count the costs properly, there was no way in which he could deliver the goods in my timescale. I badly wanted him to accept that by cutting a few corners, not too dangerously of course, we could do this thing. He could not do it. He knew it. It was wrong of me to persist with my plan as long as I did. He had the right and the duty to count the cost.

You can see people becoming less impetuous, more thoughtful and generally more careful at counting the cost of doing things in many work situations. The stock controller can become more aware of the cost of running out of items. The young researcher can become more precise in his work and avoid failures in his experiments. We can become more deliberate in making management plans. In all of these circumstances, people are counting the cost of failure. If we can combine responsible risk-taking with careful work, a great deal has been achieved. We must not see the development of those types of wisdom and insight in purely secular terms. It is almost always the case that someone gets hurt, waste occurs or some other undesirable consequence follows not counting the cost properly. Such outcomes have non–secular meanings also.

As managers, we ought to aim to take our impetuous Peters, channel their energy, teach them to count the cost, and in spite of all their tribulations and the amount of cold water poured on them, bring them to maturity.

## Things to think about

1 Qualities like impetuosity militate against the smooth running of a department. How do we react to them?
2 What costs are we not counting properly at present?
3 What are the continuing consequences of our not counting costs in the past?
4 Is our main reaction to things going wrong one of anger or getting it back onto the rails again?

## Prayer

Lord Jesus, you were able to inspire in people total commitment which led them to serve you with their whole being. But you also taught your disciples that they must count the cost of their service as well. May we never crush the commitment of people towards their work which you have given them to do by the way in which we point out the deficiencies of their approach. May we teach them how to plan and count the cost while at the same time taking reasonable risks to bring their work to completion.

*Amen*

# 10 Asleep on the Job

*'And he came and found them sleeping'* (Mark 14:37).

Jesus knew that Judas had gone out from the last supper to betray him. He wanted a little time to pray in the Garden of Gethsemane, so he told Peter, James and John how troubled he was and asked them to keep watch. Jesus was in danger since, without doubt, Judas knew the Garden and was bound to turn up sooner or later.

Knowing that they were feeling sleepy, it would have been simple for the disciples to have arranged a rota. With just a little thought, they could have done the job asked of them. When Jesus returned and found them asleep, he did chastise them just a little, but his main concern was for them. He said, 'Watch and pray, that you may not enter into temptation', and he showed understanding saying, 'The spirit is willing but the flesh is weak'. When he came back a second time, he said, 'Sleep on'.

When Judas did arrive, Peter, dear impetuous Peter, jumped in and cut off a guard's ear with his sword. Peter was having a very bad time, everything seemed to be going wrong, just as, at times, it does today. He had started by chastising Jesus for his ideas about a suffering Messiah. He cut off a guard's ear at the wrong time. He swore to stand by Jesus whatever happened and ended up denying him. He could well have done without going to sleep on the job. This episode is recorded by Mark, and since Peter gave Mark much of his Gospel material, it is clear that these events made a profound impression on his memory. Like all mistakes, Peter must have learned a lot from it.

Work demands systematic organised activity and that depends on people doing their job faithfully. Some part of most jobs are boring but they must be done. Falling asleep on such jobs is easy. As managers, we are prone to falling asleep on routine tasks such as quality control. It is easy to assume that everyone is doing their part of a project satisfactorily. Our attention is elsewhere and things are allowed to drift. The fact is that we are always falling asleep on some part of our job.

We manage frail human beings like Peter and ourselves. On the job, the state of our people varies from wide-eyed alertness to being fast asleep. When Jesus found his disciples asleep, his main concern was for them. If they kept on behaving like that, they were the ones who were going to suffer most. If our people fall asleep, is our main concern the criticism which we will receive or the harm which they are doing to themselves? If it is the latter concern, how do we deal with the problem of that man? It is difficult to point out a man's faults to him and yet leave him on the ladder, climbing upwards. Jesus did that for Peter.

I remember one occasion when I was asleep on the job. It was, and still is, very important that all the assumptions which are made on a research project are correct. If I checked nothing else, as manager I was supposed to have the experience which enabled me to put my finger on assumptions quickly. I did not even notice this one, and it was incorrect. One other person paid the price of my sleeping and for about a year his work was made very difficult.

At the end of the episode when the disciples were asleep again, and Judas arrived, we are left with the impression that Jesus was the one in charge. He knew the path which God wanted him to tread. He put the ear that Peter had cut off back on the man and made sure that the tired trio got away in safety. A manager must do likewise. He/she is responsible for anticipating what to do when things do go wrong, taking the rap if necessary and seeing that his/her employees get away and live to fight another day—even if they *were* asleep on the job.

## Things to think about

1   One of the features of the ministry of Jesus was that he took people, weak and just as they were, and made them great. Do we expect to be surrounded by supermen who never fall down on the job?
2   To what extent are we able to be calm and collected when things go wrong? Do we see that as part of our duty?
3   When did we fall asleep on a job last? What lessons did we learn?
4   When was the occasion that one of our people went to sleep on a job? Did we blow our top? What did we do and what should we have done about the project and the person?

## Prayer

Lord Jesus, in a time of great need in the Garden of Gethsemane three of your trusted disciples went to sleep. They could have learned many things in that Garden. Teach us to be aware of the temptation to let our attention wander and forget important parts of the jobs which you give us to do. Teach us to deal constructively with those who do fall asleep on the jobs which we give them to do. Help us to remain calm and in control when things do go wrong.

*Amen*

# 11 Incredible Bravery

*'Then he began to invoke a curse on himself and to swear, "I do not know the man"'* (Matthew 26:74).

Peter's threefold denial of Jesus covers up one of the bravest acts recorded in the New Testament. When Jesus was being questioned, following his arrest, Peter was in the inner courtyard of the High Priest's house, a very dangerous place in which to be. Two servant girls had already recognised him, but he stayed. Some men came up and recognised him, maybe due to his Galilean accent, and they would have been much more likely to press the matter than the girls. We are told that Peter swore that he did not know Jesus and asked God to punish him if this were not so.

Whatever danger Peter might have been in, he had stayed in that courtyard. Cocks were not allowed in that part of Jerusalem because they would defile the area. 'Cockcrow' was a name given to the 3 *am* Roman trumpet call and, since night finished at 6 *am*, Peter had been there most of the night. It must have taken a lot of courage to go there in the first place. To have stayed so long shows his extreme attachment and loyalty to Jesus. The story goes on to tell how Peter remembered Jesus' words and then went away and wept. The New Testament draws a discreet veil over his agony and torment.

As managers, having launched some work, we usually withdraw and come back in on its final stages to see how successful it has been. Things do not go wrong very often, but what is our reaction when they do? When we are in the midst of a battle and obviously losing, what do we think of a colleague who turns tail and runs for safety? What do we do when he starts to deny all knowledge of our plans if he gets into a tight corner? What do we do when one of our lieutenants panics and starts to do all sorts of foolish things? Peter was a man of panic.

Perhaps because we are men, it is inevitable that our first reaction will be one of anger. But our second one ought to be to recollect the ways in which that man has stood by us in the past. When we were last in difficulties, probably due to our own bad judgment, was he the person who stood by us, took some of the knocks and eventually helped us to deal with the situation? How often have we pushed him into the firing line to take some of the brunt of our battles? We ought to remember such things.

Another issue to consider is, 'How did he get into that position in the first place?' Were we responsible for misjudging his present abilities? Did we prepare him for this battle and should we have been by his side winning that battle with him and for him? Was it fair to get him into that exposed position? What must he have felt like when he started to do that job and what did he feel about the final mess? Metaphorically speaking, has he been weeping?

Once, at my place of work, we changed a system by which priorities on work were set. The arguments which led to that decision were complex and of little relevance. There came a point when we had to face the gathered armies of those from whom we were removing a great deal of power. Hostility was written all over their faces. The analogy breaks down at that point because my right hand man was taken into that battle by me. He panicked and I had to cut him out of the action completely because he could not stand the sort of pressure to which he was exposed. But, he had come with me. The main fault was my error of judgment, not his panic.

If one of our people does panic, our first reaction might be anger, but our second one ought to be gratitude that they were brave enough to be there in the first place.

## Things to think about

1  When did we last feel 'denied' by one of our own people? Why do we think we behaved in that way?
2  How did he get into that position? How responsible were we for his problem? List the ways he has stood by us in the past.
3  When did we panic last and deny our part in some action? How do we feel about that now?
4  How careful are we about assessing people's ability to take responsibility and to deal with difficult situations? Do we give it a thought?

## Prayer

Lord Jesus, we thank you for all our colleagues who, because of their faithfulness and bravery, have stood by us in the past. Help us to remember their good qualities when we are most affected by their weaknesses. Grant that, whether by mis-judgment or for any other cause, we may never place them in positions which are beyond their capabilities. If they panic, give us the understanding and ability to help them.

*Amen*

# 12  A Message for Peter

*'And he said to them, "Do not be amazed; you seek Jesus of Nazareth, who was crucified. He has risen, he is not here; see the place where they laid him. But go, tell his disciples and Peter that he is going before you to Galilee"'* (Mark 16:6).

Around about the time that Jesus was crucified, things were not going well for Peter. His denial of Jesus had been the culmination of that series of happenings, a denial which he made three times. For Peter, the man who first recognised that Jesus was God's Messiah, the cross must have been a shattering experience. Peter must have reached one of those all-time lows in which he was going through one of those heart-rending, once-in-a-lifetime periods of depression. He had been with Jesus for three years, put all his faith and hopes in him, and it all ended up with a common criminal type of execution—a crucifixion. What would we have felt like in Peter's place?

Jesus knew that Peter would deny him. Jesus understood men and he knew that Peter would be at an all-time low. So Peter got a very special mention when the message about the resurrection was sent out to the disciples. 'Tell Peter' was an order full of compassion. That special message shows just how concerned Jesus was for Peter in the middle of these traumatic events. With skill and sympathy, Jesus picked up Peter and put him back on his feet again.

Whatever sort of department we run, we have a small, tight band of people around us on whom we rely to get things done. Those people will have many different qualities and it is quite likely that there is someone like Peter among them. Creative management is about doing things that have never been done before and taking that group through unexplored, uncharted territory in order to do those new things. Misunderstanding what we are doing, the need to switch tack quickly, outright failure of nerve and a thousand other reasons, cause some of our small band of followers to stumble. Some of those stumbles by colleagues are minor diversions which we take in our stride. Others are more serious. For example, what do you do about the colleague who panics, abandons an agreed plan and then runs for cover. Our small band will contain someone who will do that sort of thing at some time.

If we are good managers and have a little good fortune, we will win through and then we are faced with what to do about Peter. It is not very easy to send our Peter a special message. It is much easier to feel a great deal of resentment and to feel badly hurt by the whole process. There are practical problems as well. Just what do we do when a very sheepish Peter reappears for the first time? The important thing about this Bible story is that, no matter how much it cost, Jesus took the initiative. He must have had quite a good idea about the state of mind that Peter would have been in by that time. His 'special message' was a generous and considerate action but, above all, it was simple, direct, personal and immediate.

There is another message in this story about Peter's all-time low which should not be missed. Peter's weeping must have been due, at least in part, to his own view of his own worthlessness and failure. We should be sensitive about the feelings of uselessness and worthlessness which others are experiencing and which are causing them to feel depressed. It is not God's will for a man that he should feel worthless. Just as Jesus made this clear to Peter, we have a similar duty to our people. We should be aware of all the 'special messages' that we need to give to others.

## Things to think about

1  When did we last feel badly let down by one of our people? How did we feel about it?
2  Have we dealt with a member of our staff after such an occasion? How did we do it?
3  Are there people around us to whom we should be sending generous special messages?
4  Mistakes teach people important things in life. How does our organisation deal with the bad patches through which people go? Do we try to make them a learning experience?

## Prayer

Lord Jesus, Peter could not see the path which you were following and, despite his faithfulness and bravery, he made mistakes. You dealt with him generously, lifted him up gently and set him on his road again. When we feel most let down by colleagues, give us a generous mind and make their well-being our chief concern. When we know how despondent they feel about their actions, give us the skill to help to set them on their feet once more.

*Amen*

# 13  A Committed Follower

*'Jesus said to Simon Peter, "Simon, son of John, do you love me more than these?"'* (John 21:15).

There are some scenes in the Bible story which must have been indelibly inscribed for the rest of their lives on the memories of those who were there. Peter can never have forgotten this one. Some time after the resurrection, Jesus was out in a boat with some disciples and he asked Peter this question. We do not know what or who 'these' referred to. Jesus could have meant the people around or the fishing gear and boats or something else. We do not know. What we do know is that Jesus asked for love and he asked for it three times.

Jesus could have asked all sorts of questions. 'Do you repent?' 'Will you follow me?' Instead he asked, 'Do you love me?' Jesus had spent a large proportion of his ministry redefining the word 'love'. His disciples had heard his revolutionary definition of love in the story of the Good Samaritan. The Samaritans were lower than the lowest of the low in the eyes of the Jew and yet Jesus had chosen one of them to tell a pharisee how and whom he must love. By his death for mankind on the cross, Jesus had redefined love again in terms of God's love for man. The power and the love defined on the cross were sufficient to convert the whole known world in a relatively short time. And yet, Jesus asked Peter, 'Do you love me?'

Jesus had been denied by Peter three times and Jesus asked Peter 'Do you love me?' three times. It is as if he was allowing Peter to wash away his denials one at a time by three amazing declarations of commitment. Peter committed himself to Jesus right up to the hilt. It was that commitment that took him to his cross in Rome. Jesus asked for and got the ultimate in commitment from Peter — a commitment called love.

If we read any management literature or talk about how things are going at work, we will soon get onto the topics like commitment and motivation. In very crude terms, management theory breaks down into two types—the scientific and the human relations type. A very high percentage of the human relations type is concerned with how people feel about their job, the way they are treated and their individual commitment to their work. That theory always raises in my mind one important question. Just how great a commitment to his job are we entitled to ask from a man?

Once, I had the job of managing a very exciting research project. If it was a success and we could spread the results, the implications were enormous. We were a very small, tight-knit band of five. For 15 months, we almost lived together 24 hours a day. The project was based on one of my ideas, but it developed quickly and became the property of all of us. Everyone became totally committed to that work. I have never had that same level of commitment from any other team over such a long period. I asked a great deal from that team and they gave me everything I asked. Was I right in asking for that commitment?

We all know that there are no easy answers to that question. In a research department it is common to find a group of young people, often unmarried, who seem to live for their work. There seems to be little to criticise in the situation. On the other hand, there is a lot to criticise when we see a middle-aged man's legitimate interests in and responsibilities for his family being displaced by his job. As managers, are we being fair when we allow work to play havoc with a man's life? The annual plan that consumes weeks of work, day and night, creates chaos and generally disrupts every other activity in sight—have we a legitimate right to ask that from people? Do we camouflage our own inability to manage in terms of 'esprit de corps' and 'being the best' and so on? Just what do we have the right to ask?

Jesus asked Peter three times for the greatest commitment on earth. He did not snatch that commitment, Peter gave it freely. Jesus had earned that commitment on the cross. He earns it now by the service which he gives to men before he asks anything in return. He earns it now by the way he stands by his followers and workers. He earns it when, through the Holy Spirit, he gives them the resources they need. Every manager worth his salt knows that the commitment we ask from others has got to be earned. It has got to be reasonable in terms of the facilities which we provide. Above all, it is not reasonable to demand from others that they compensate for our lack of service to them by their overstretching themselves for us.

We are not entitled to ask from others the commitment of love which Jesus asked and received from Peter. We should ask ourselves frequently what we have earned by our service to them before we think of making demands on them.

## Things to think about

1   What is our attitude towards the commitment that we ask from others? Is it something that our organisation has paid for and is therefore ours by right? Or do we have to earn it?
2   If commitment that is freely given is worth more than the sort we pay for, what are the basic processes of earning and giving that commitment?
3   Have we a duty to limit the commitment that we demand so that colleagues can meet their other legitimate demands?
4   Think of a specific case in which we have not succeeded in establishing the appropriate level of commitment in someone. What went wrong?

5   Think of someone who is definitely over-committed. What are the consequences of that and how do we start to correct the situation?

## Prayer

Lord Jesus, we thank you for the example of Peter's love for you and for your example of how to earn that love. Teach us that there is a right level of commitment that we have a duty to earn when we need it from our colleagues. If our people are under-committed to their work, help us to see their problems. If they are over-committed, to the extent of neglecting other duties, may we recognise and correct that situation and see our own fault in allowing it to happen.

*Amen*

# 14  Towards Responsibility

*'In those days, Peter stood up'* (Acts 1:15).

The Acts of the Apostles is the story of one of the most gripping projects in the Bible—the spread of the Gospel throughout the ancient world. Peter played a major part in that project and, for anyone who studies that part, this must be one of the most thrilling verses in Acts. From now on, Jesus was working through people who served him. If we are members of the Church, then there is an established pattern showing the way Jesus has worked over the last two thousand years. But Peter did not have that pattern. He started from next to nothing. Here was the man who had started his service by pushing his boat out from the shore, a simple fisherman, a man who had both his high spots and his low spots when Jesus was alive, here was that same man getting up on his own two feet and starting to organise the work of the Church. This was a tremendous moment.

A short time later, in Acts 2:14, Peter stood up again and preached the Gospel to outsiders. That time, Peter and the young Church were both well and truly on their way.

We should always be thrilled when we see someone take up the reins and start to go places. As managers, we have that thrill very often. The junior who has just taken their first piece of shorthand has grown. The senior executive who has just made his/her first board-room presentation has developed. It does not matter whether the person concerned is the most junior office girl or the most senior manager—we should always be glad. We should be thrilled. We should show our joy and our pleasure to that person. If we have taught someone to be a bigger person, that is a marvellous thing to have done. If someone else has done that teaching for us, we should be truly grateful.

It should be one of our constant concerns to discover how we can help our own people to do their next lot of standing on their own two feet. We should know the sort of things that we want them to be doing at various stages in their careers. The man in his mid-twenties who has just been given his first project is about to start growing. The 30 year old who has been given wider project re-sponsibilities is growing. The 40 year old who is just about to run the works is growing. Every person who is about to do a new thing is growing and we should never lose the excitement, thrill and joy of seeing that happen. We should be particularly glad when the wise, mature person steps up to take major responsibility, even when, and especially when, that means that one of our own people has overtaken us on the ladder.

We should always remember that the Peter who stood up on this occasion was the same Peter who had fallen down at other times. Jesus did a great job putting Peter back on his feet until the time came when Peter was able to stand himself.

## Things to think about

1  Just how good are we at recognising and giving praise enthu-siastically when people stand up on their own two feet? When did we last do it?
2  What preparation are we making and what risks are we pre-pared to take so that our own people can mature? Think about some particular person for whom this is not going well. What are we doing wrong?
3  What was the latest occasion when we refused to stand on our own feet? What are the continuing consequences?
4  What is our policy in this field? Do we plan to move people into more responsible positions sufficiently carefully?

## Prayer

Lord Jesus, we thank you that Peter stood up, took responsibility and gave us an example to follow. May we and our people grow to maturity in a like manner.

*Amen*

# 15 Prejudices

*'Rise Peter; kill and eat'* (Acts 10:13).

One of the great miracles which is recorded in Acts is the transformation of Christianity from a Jewish sect into a world religion. Jesus told his disciples to take the Gospel to the end of the world. As the Gentiles started to join the Church, it became increasingly clear that the Jewish Law was a major stumbling block for them. This particular verse is concerned with the Jewish food laws but the problem was much more widespread. The Law, as described in the first five books of the Bible, was the very essence of Judaism. Its position in Christian circles was completely changed in the early years of the Church and, for a Jew like Peter, that must have been a traumatic experience.

It is difficult for us, after two thousand years, to put ourselves in the place of those early Jewish Christians. The Law was not a source of drudgery or a set of rather odd limitations for the Jew. In the Psalms we read, 'Oh, how I love thy Law! It is my meditation all the day' (Psalm 119:97). The Psalms are full of praise and thankfulness for the Law. The relationship which the devout Jew had with his God through the Law brought him strength and hope, peace and pleasure. Peter was a true Jew and when he was told in his dream to kill and eat that which was unclean, he must have been absolutely amazed and appalled. For Peter to change from that view was a miracle. We should never underestimate the personal change which Peter made when he displaced the Law from the central position in his life and made it possible for the Church to carry on with its mission to the Gentiles.

The way things were done in Jewish society was influenced greatly by the Jewish Law. In a similar way, the climate of our organisation is fashioned by fundamental attitudes which we hold, and that climate determines the things which we can do usefully. For example, our attitude towards change influences whether or not it is sensible to send people away to learn new techniques. When they return with new ideas, do we really want to know about those ideas and do we seek to use them? Is our prejudice against new methods such that it is positively dishonest and unhelpful to raise people's hopes and their vision by sending them away on these courses? We will find it difficult to admit that some of our own attitudes do have these characteristics and are prejudices, but it is probably true.

In the depths of the 1979–1981 depression, companies could pick and choose which new graduates they hired — there was no shortage. Some major companies couched their advertisements in tough, aggressive terms. One would have thought that a would-be employee had to be tough and ruthless with an ability to remove any obstacle from his chosen course of action no matter who or what was in the way. Maybe this was just an advertising gimmick but maybe it did represent the value system which those companies had adopted at that time. When we recruit someone and process him through our training scheme, we are going to change his value system. When we promote him, we expect him to adopt a little more of our way of life. When we give him responsibility we expect him to promote our way of life and our climate. Do we ask ourselves sufficiently often and sufficiently pointedly just what our climate, our ethos and culture is based on?

Just what are our basic rules? Does our organisation care anything about its employees? All that stuff in our recruitment leaflets extolling the virtues of our company—does it reflect reality? Is it honest? Do we mind how we get our business? How do we intend to carve out our market position over the next few years? How are we going to put our old, old 'has-beens' 'out to grass'? Does cutthroat competition justify anything we care to do? What are the issues which determine the sort of place that we run? The answers to these sort of questions are not the basis for some sort of irrelevant philosophical report or thesis. They determine our way of life in a minute-by-minute sense, just as the Jewish Law determined the way of the life of Peter.

Peter was right to refuse to change his way of life without a lot of thought. Before we start changing the life that we have, we ought to understand what it is that we have now. It may well be that after careful consideration we do believe that God would have us behave very differently but we should be prepared to defend that which we have worked out over a lifetime rather than change it with every wind that blows. Change for the sake of change is not a good idea. However, it is possible that we are in Peter's position, being asked to make major changes, if only we had the ability to understand the consequences of our present position.

## Things to think about

1   Are we aware of our own ingrained behaviour patterns or are such things only possessed by other people in our eyes? List the ones we have — carefully.

2    When did we last make a major change to our important be-
     haviour patterns? Why did we do it? Should we have made a
     change which, for some reason, we managed to avoid?
3    Peter must have loved the Jewish way of life, its Law and
     its customs. Name something in our work life which we love
     in the same way? What would be our reaction if that were
     challenged?
4    What old ways at work are we sticking to with the tenacity of a
     bulldog? Are we being wise in behaving in that way? Are we
     aware of any challenges to those beliefs or are we being blind to
     all challengers?

## Prayer

Lord Jesus, you taught Peter the Jew to question those beliefs
which he held dear, and you led him eventually to change them
and to make possible a whole new way of life for the young
Church. We thank you that you are able to open people's eyes in
this way. Teach us to know those beliefs which we hold most dear.
Help us to question them when they get in the way of change. But
equally, help us to hold fast to those which are good and worth
preserving.

*Amen*

# 16  Building the Kingdom

*'[Herod] killed James the brother of John with the sword; and when he saw
that it pleased the Jews, he proceeded to arrest Peter also'* (Acts 12:1).

Jesus never pretended that building the Kingdom was an easy job, a
job for someone who really wanted to be left alone to sit in his easy
chair by the fire. Many parts of the story of Peter illustrate his
courage and the fight which the young Church and Peter put up in
order to spread the Gospel. This episode concerns one of the
Herods, several of whom are mentioned in the New Testament.
None of them appear to have been men of high principle. Perhaps a
local king like the Herods in a tiny unimportant corner of the
Roman Empire could not afford principles: we do not know.
Clearly Luke, the writer of the Acts, believed that this Herod
was badly in need of some local Jewish support, saw a cheap way of
getting it and proceeded to deal with Peter accordingly. Good men
will recognise and at least tolerate a Godly act. Opposition will

often come from unpleasant characters like Herod who have local power but are often in fundamentally weak positions. God delivered Peter out of the hands of Herod in due course. But in worldly terms, he did not deliver James, brother of John.

According to Acts, Peter escaped from jail in a miraculous way and fled the country. Although it is not impossible for us to be jailed for our managerial activities, it is unlikely. Our fights with men like Herod are likely to be less spectacular and so are our escapes.

The actual course of this incident in the young Church is relevant to today's workplaces. Herod needed to bolster up his position, in other words, to curry favour. Someone's need to curry favour is always a dangerous situation. Peter Drucker suggests that we often promote managers beyond their capacities and capabilities and this puts them in a weak position. The good foreman often makes a poor junior manager and the good researcher often makes a bad research director. In their weakness, these people are vulnerable. In their weakness, such people may buy their own security, sometimes unknowingly, by treating colleagues less than fairly. Sometimes such people have no alternative but to seek to curry favour.

In a public service, what do you do when you see the old, the mentally handicapped or the psychogeriatrics getting less than their fair share of the budget. Powerful people run expensive, shrewd services so that they can use as much money as they are able to get. Managers need the support of those people very often and cannot fight them continuously. In industry, a local authority may curry favour with a large, rich, powerful company with money to invest, by giving it sites which are needed by the community for other purposes. All sorts of spurious arguments about the economic value of such services or the better economic growth which will result from using that particular site will be put forward to justify the actions, but the real reason will be Herod's—the need to curry favour.

Peter had developed the strength to fight his battles, a strength given to him by God. He had come a long way since he had joined Jesus back in Galilee. Soberly and with great courage, Peter was fighting the battles of the Kingdom against men like Herod. We must expect to have to do likewise. Work is part of that battlefield.

## Things to think about

1   Who are the Herods in our life, the people with power who will

do anything to retain and enhance their own status and influence?

2 Peter preached despite Herod. Are we being asked to do something, no matter how small, for God, like this? How do we prepare to do it?

3 Peter's development route from Galilee to Rome went through some difficult periods and such episodes teach people a great deal. What difficulties at work are we trying to overcome at present?

4 God intervened to deliver Peter. What part is God playing in our development at the moment?

## Prayer

Lord Jesus, you led Peter through difficult situations and he became one of your great servants. Grant that we may recognise the difficult things which you give us to do for you and give us the strength to do them.

*Amen*

# 17 A Saint

*'Truly, truly, I say to you, when you were young, you girded yourself and walked where you would; but when you are old, you will stretch out your hands, and another will gird you and carry you where you do not wish to go'* (John 21:18).

Church tradition suggests that Peter, the simple Galilean fisherman, was crucified in Rome in fulfilment of this prophecy by Jesus. His life and career development sanctified Peter, caused him to be set apart in his service to God, caused him to become a saint. As we trace the career of Peter through his days with Jesus, watch him in the days around the death and resurrection of Jesus, stay with him as he built up the young Church and agreed to its going out to the Gentile world, in all that wonderful career we see a man who is truly growing towards 'the fullness of the stature of Christ'. It is easy to believe that his death on a cross, just like that of his own Lord and Master, made his service as near perfect as a man will ever get.

Jesus does not ask that level of service from most of us; we would not make the grade. He does ask that two talents be made four, and five be transformed into ten. He does ask that we try to define the goals which he is setting for us and that we pursue those goals diligently and with the considerable help which he gives to us.

As managers, we sit down frequently and work out our goals. Our goals must be practical ones, but that is no reason to pretend that they are unimportant to God. If we give a service to others, that service should be fashioned on the service which Jesus gave to us. If we fashion a product, it should be the best because we use God's material to make it. Our honesty must be beyond reproach. Our dealings with people should recognise that they are our neighbours, children of our common Heavenly Father, who possess an absolute right to our loving care for them.

Our ultimate goal as managers is to serve other people and the organisation for which we work. We are not given our positions to serve only ourselves and gratify our own ego. The model for that service is Jesus himself and his service to God. That model took Peter to his death on a cross. We might not scale those heights, but we should not settle for some shoddy compromise which is far less than the goal which God gave us the ability and the strength to reach.

## Things to think about

1  Have we ever set down what managing right up to God's highest standard would be like?
2  Write down the most important things we do. How do we transform each of those into a service worthy of being offered to God, *ie* true worship?
3  If Peter's readiness to go to his death is our true model of service to God, how do we teach that to people around us?
4  Pick a person—how do we teach him to serve others like Peter and how do we show him the rewards of such service?

## Prayer

Lord Jesus, you took Peter, the fisherman, and taught him and moulded him. You gave him strength to lead the Church and ultimately to sacrifice his life in your service. Teach us never to be satisfied with giving a lesser service than, with your power, we are able. Show us how to increase that service day by day in our work.

*Amen*

# 18
# A Prayer for a Follower

Lord Jesus,

You called Peter to your service;
> teach us never to recruit anyone until we have a job for them which has been thought out carefully.

You gave Peter a job worth doing and explained it to him in terms which he understood;
> teach us never to create jobs which do not offer people the chance of fulfilment and which they themselves do not understand.

You brought Peter back onto the right road gently but firmly;
> teach us to see our own mistakes and to show others their mistakes with a concern for their own well-being.

You dealt gently with Peter's impulsiveness;
> teach us to accept and to work with the faults of ourselves and others and to find ways of overcoming them.

You inspired in Peter a fundamental commitment to your cause;
> teach us to give people work to which they can commit an appropriate portion of their lives and find their joy in it.

You upheld Peter when his faith faltered;
> teach us to reassure and give strength to people when they cannot see the point of their work.

You remained in command when Peter fell asleep;
> teach us to look for the reasons when we seem to fail badly and to allow for the weaknesses of people in our plans.

You accepted in a kindly way Peter's commitment to follow you even to death, knowing that he could not yet do that;
> teach us to accept the over-enthusiasm of others in a kindly but critical way.

You caused Peter to grow, to stand and to do great things;
  teach us to develop each gift in ourselves and in others.

You showed Peter how to overcome his prejudices and serve you
      better;
  teach us not to be blinded by our own beliefs and to help
  overcome the short-sightedness of others.

You enabled Peter to face danger in the work which you gave him
      to do;
  teach us to face up to problems at work and to encourage and
  strengthen others in their difficulties.

You made Peter into a saint;
  teach us to grow towards the fullness of the stature of Christ and
  to enable others to do the same.

*Amen*

# Part II
# Power

# 19
# Making Things Happen

There is something that is not quite nice about power. It is something that we do not talk about too much. Yet, even if we are a comparatively junior manager, we have a great deal of power. If we are senior people, then we make many decisions concerned with a wide variety of issues and we have the power to make our decision stick should anyone attempt to go against them. Our decisions and our power are two of the basic parts of our job.

If we were to examine management literature to discover how much has been written about power, we should find not much of it refers to operational management situations. That literature is starting to grow, mainly as social scientists turn their attention in that direction. This small amount of theory is supplemented by biographical material about the great characters of modern industry and various exposés of the misuse of power, but even with the addition of this material, there is not a great deal from which we can learn. Political power has a much more extensive literature and reading about national figures and their exercise of power is very worthwhile. But the basic picture remains. Maybe because of the wide variety of contexts within which power is exercised, managers will be hard pressed to find widely accepted, usable theories of the power they possess.

Christianity, like its predecessor Judaism, is an action-orientated religion, a religion about doing things in accordance with the will of God. Action presupposes that the power to act exists and the Bible is full of examples of God using his power in this world. Our use of the several varieties of power which we possess must be shaped by our understanding of the way God uses power and wants it used in this world. We must exercise our power responsibly and with humility. The fact that it is not regarded as nice to talk about power—and that our models and understanding of its use are inadequate—does not absolve us from examining critically our own use of power. We cannot evade this duty.

# 20  Models of Management Power

*'Let every person be subject to the governing authorities. For there is no authority except from God, and those that exist have been instituted by God'* (Romans 13:1).

It is only in comparatively recent times that powerful organisations other than nation states, empires and religious bodies have developed. The modern company or public authority exercise considerable power. Some of these companies have more money available to them and a larger turnover than a reasonably sized state. If Paul had known of such entities, there is little doubt that he would have included them alongside 'authorities' in this verse. Paul would have maintained that the authority and power which exists within our modern organisations came from God just as much as the type of organisational power which he knew.

Apart from the principle that all power comes from God, the Bible has one other prevalent theme allied to the use of power, namely that people are much more important than property and material things in general. In the Old Testament, the laws relating to wrongs done against people are much more severe in tone than those relating to material things. As far as our use of power affects people rather than property, we carry a greater responsibility and our actions must be better considered.

Apart from these two great principles the Bible does not seem to contain an elaborate theory of power. However, such a theory is implied by the many action–orientated episodes recorded in it. It would be quite wrong to overlook these illustrations of the use of power if we are trying to put together a basis for our own action. In particular we should note that these action–orientated episodes illustrate the fundamental nature of our God. Other religions place emphasis on the nature of God and men contemplating that nature. The Christian God is an interventionist God of action. We cannot evade taking action if we follow such a God. That means we need to have some understanding of power.

In recent years, management scientists have given much thought to the analysis of power. One of the best known of these modern theories is a five type model developed by J P P French (J P P French and B Raven, *The Basis of Social Power*, Cartwright and Zander, Group Dynamics, Tavistock, 1960). His five types are:

(i)   the power to give rewards of various types;
(ii)  power derived from our being referred to;

(iii) the power to coerce and punish;

(iv) legitimised power due to our position in a hierarchy; and

(v) the expert power we have through possessing special knowledge.

As managers we can recognise these modern types of power quite easily. We use them all. We need to reconcile these modern models which we recognise and use with the more fundamental biblical models. Expert power and the other four types of power are still powers delegated to us from God. If our actions influence people, our love relationship to them is still paramount, whether our actions are based on legitimate power or any other sort of power. No matter what sort of power our actions use, they are only acceptable as far as they reflect God's desired action in this world.

As managers, one of our distinguishing features is that we possess more power than those for whom we are responsible. The fundamental biblical position is that, whatever modern model we use to describe that power, it comes from God and is for use in his service.

## Things to think about

1   List some of the things we have done recently which demonstrate the power which we have been given. Were we aware of taking those actions using God's delegated power?

2   In what sense did each of those actions represent the will of God in that situation? If it did not do so, how could our action be improved?

3   Name the ways in which our actions have affected specific people. Did we give those actions special consideration? How could our actions have been improved?

4   In the next few days, our actions will require our use of our power. In what ways can we make those actions more Godly?

## Prayer

Lord Jesus, we have been taught to pray 'Our Father, Thine is the Power'. Give us a firm commitment to exercise all the power which you have given us in accordance with God's will for us and for those around us.

*Amen*

# 21  The Power to Reward

*'Your reward is great in heaven'* (Matthew 5:12).

There is a slightly nasty tinge about the idea of a reward, at least when we are in one of our high-minded moods. We tend to put a higher value on work which is done for no payment. Yet the idea of a reward has deep roots in the Gospel message. The labourer is said to be worthy of his hire. The men who use their talents are given more. Paul loves his similes and metaphors concerned with races and prizes. All this reflects the very nature of God. In Matthew 7:11, we are told that God knows how to give good gifts to those who ask. Ultimately, we are told, 'Your reward is great in heaven'.

Rewarding people is an intrinsic part of management. In many instances, we have the power to decide the actual monetary reward within very wide limits. In other cases, we can select only the scale on which someone will be rewarded. We tend to regard discussions about salaries and wages as necessary chores but we do not look forward to them. We should remember that, as well as being a good socialist slogan, 'A fair day's work for a fair day's pay' is a Godly one as well. If we have lost our interest in a fair and just monetary reward for our people, then we have forgotten a duty.

Monetary rewards are not the only ones which we give to people and many management scientists doubt whether they are the most important. Status, the prize tasks and words of praise are some of the other rewards which we can give. Although not quite rewards, we do give people many other things as well. These include our consideration, our kindness, our various contributions to the atmosphere in which they work and things specific to particular occasions, such as our undivided attention. The whole work experience of a person can be more or less rewarding according to the actions which we, as managers, decide to take. As managers, we have considerable power to shape that experience and to withhold rewards or reflect the generosity of our Heavenly Father and the way in which he rewards people.

One of the things about a reward which we should remember is that it must be earned. St Paul's famous races had to be run and the prizes had to be won. The man who turns in distinctly mediocre work, well beneath his capacity, does not deserve a reward. It may be that a sharp rap on the knuckles is a more Godly response to his efforts, that may do him much more good. Power can be used to give or to withhold rewards and we have a duty to decide which course to take.

One of our main concerns as managers is the way in which a person moves towards his own maturity. We influence that path by our rewards to him. We have the power to fashion those incentives, a power given to us by God. At the very least, it can be shown that incentives and rewards were part of the way in which Jesus and New Testament writers thought about life in the Kingdom of God. That fact should cause us to reflect on the way we use rewards on earth, especially at work.

## Things to think about

1   What is our basic reaction to the concept of reward?
2   What are the rewards which we have the power to give to others on a regular basis? How many have we given out this week?
3   Do people find work in our department a rewarding experience? What specific things should we be doing to make this more true?
4   Given that money does form a major part of our earthly reward system, and given the dangers that are associated with the possession of money, how do we react to these modern incentive systems?

## Prayer

Lord Jesus, you taught us that our generous Heavenly Father loves to reward and to give good gifts to his children. Teach us to understand more fully the rewards which we can give to others and teach us to use them wisely.

*Amen*

# 22  A Point of Reference

*'If I then, your Lord and Teacher has washed your feet, you also ought to wash one another's feet'* (John 13:13).

When we become managers, we usually move out of the job of actually producing the goods which our company sells. We become organisers very often. We are looked to for our wide knowledge of the work being done and our ability to solve problems. People start to refer to us for all sorts of different things and the advice and guidance which we give makes up a major part of our power.

There are two ways by which people refer to us: by asking for help and by watching us. Most of us recognise our own short-comings and would much rather that people asked us what to do and did what we told them to do. But life is not like that. People watch us and are influenced much more by our actions than by our words. Of course, our words do matter, but they only carry the full weight of our position and power when they are at one with the image which our life projects to others.

If we are referred to in these two ways, just what sort of image goes across to others? One possible image is that of a pompous ass, full of our own importance, probably quite knowledgeable, but prone to being self-opinionated and to directing rather than to leading others. Our knowledge and our position combine to force others to refer to us but they do not do it gladly or willingly. There are several other possible models and one of them must bear some resemblance to Jesus washing the disciples' feet.

The person who washed a visitor's feet in a Jewish household was carrying out one of the most menial jobs in that house. He was getting near to giving the ultimate in service in some ways. How do we serve others best when they refer to us? The first thing we ought to do is to find out what piece of advice they actually want. Obvious perhaps, but seldom taken seriously as a problem. Listening to someone else attentively is hard work. It is much easier if they just listen to us prattle on, even if we miss the point of their question. A true servant is courteous also. Even if our questioner is rather foolish, not to say rather stupid, he still has a right to basic courtesy. Even if our advice has been given a thousand times before, we should not seem to belittle that person. To be in posses-sion of power and to be referred to by others gives us an oppor-tunity to serve others, not to lord it over them.

Jesus had more power and status than we will ever possess. Yet, in so many ways, like this incident with the towel, he set out to serve others. It is a privilege when others seek our advice and guidance and we must set out to serve others just as Jesus did.

## Things to think about

1   Name the occasions when we were referred to recently. How did we play each occasion?
2   What sort of issues do people bring to us regularly? What sort of image do we project at those times?

3 Do we accept that people refer to us most often by following our example? Analyse that example.
4 How well does the example we set reflect the service which God would have us give?

## Prayer

Lord Jesus, when people looked to you in your earthly life for advice and for help, you met their need and you served them. When people come to us for help and advice, may we meet their need and serve them in the same way.

*Amen*

# 23 The Power to Coerce

*'And as they led him away, they seized one Simon of Cyrene, who was coming in from the country, and laid on him the cross, to carry it behind Jesus'* (Luke 23:26).

Jesus was on his way to Calvary. The centurion who was leading the execution party would have had orders to take him by the longest route to impress upon the population the might of Rome and the fate which befell wrongdoers. That centurion had the power to press anyone into the service of the state just by touching his shoulder with the tip of his spear. When Jesus grew tired, such was the fate of Simon. He was probably a Jew, up from the country, in Jerusalem for his once-in-a-lifetime celebration of the Passover in the Holy City. When power was used to coerce Simon into this particular service, his sense of frustration, resentment and hatred of the Romans must have been at an all-time high. All coercion causes people to have such feelings.

As managers, we know that we do not generate in people a perfect understanding of what we wish to do every time we act. We know that not everyone falls in behind our lead happily and with full commitment. There are many reasons for this state of affairs. It takes time to persuade people to do what we want and sometimes we do not have time. Many of our actions are politically based and it is sometimes not expedient for others to know our reasons fully. Some people, for a variety of reasons, simply would not understand no matter how long we spent telling them about our reasons. We are not saints and sometimes we do not feel like telling everyone why we want to do something. After all, we are managers, and we are paid to act and get things done!

Sometimes managers have no alternative to coercion. Once during work on one of our projects, two of my colleagues came to me with radically different methods of taking that work forward. I failed to get them to agree and I had to make a choice. One of these people, according to the rule book, was slightly more senior to the other, but he was not his manager. Eventually I decided that we should go down the path suggested by the less senior colleague. That decision caused bitter resentment. I ended up having to guide that project to its conclusion with an iron hand. That was coercion. If we are managers, we all do this at sometime.

As the years have passed, a manager's ability to coerce someone else into action has been reduced. Sacking someone is no longer the simple process it used to be. It is true that most of us have specific disciplinary procedures available to us if our orders are not obeyed, but it is often time-consuming in the extreme to use them. On the whole we tend to get round such situations by involving others in the decisions and obtaining their commitment to them. Nowadays, we tend to be followed for our knowledge, our insight and our ability to get things done.

Although it may be true that outright coercion does not feature much in modern management, we are still expected to give a positive lead. A dithering manager is a menace. At the far extreme from the person who acts always by imposing their will is the person who will not move an inch if anyone is even tending to disagree with them. Maybe it is not the will of God that we should take away all semblance of freedom from a man by coercion. But neither is it the will of God that we should stand by in a bemused, helpless state when a colleague tries to turn his freedom into a licence to disrupt all creative, social action in a workplace. Somehow, we must steer between these two extremes using one of God's most precious gifts to us—wisdom.

There is a possible story behind the Simon of Cyrene episode. Mark, who wrote his Gospel in Rome, describes a Simon who was the father of Alexander and Rufus. In Paul's letter to Rome, he greets 'Rufus, eminent in the Lord, also his mother and mine' (Romans 16:13). If it is the same Simon, it is clear that Paul thought a great deal of Simon's family. Maybe the coercion of Simon led to a happy ending. If we believe that a way forward is the right way, then we must use the power given to us to follow that path and if the road is rather bumpy, we must leave the outcome in God's hands.

## Things to think about

1 When did we last use our power to impose our way forward on an unwilling colleague? How did we feel about that action?
2 When were we last in a state of dithering indecision? What did we do and how do we feel about that action now?
3 What is our management style? Do we tend to coerce and give a strong lead? Are we right?
4 How far would we go to avoid even covert coercion? How near do our other management characteristics push us towards coercion?

## Prayer

Lord Jesus, we remember Simon of Cyrene who was pressed into service to carry your cross to Calvary. Teach us to be sensitive and to know when we are forcing people to act against their will. When we believe that such actions are our only course, help us to mini-mise the hurt and the resentment which they must feel. May we remember always to put the outcome of such actions in your hands.

*Amen*

# 24 Legitimate Power

*'As soon as it was morning, the chief priests, with the elders and scribes, and the whole council held a consultation, and they bound Jesus and led him away and delivered him to Pilate'* (Mark 15:1).

Legitimate power is that power which an organisation confers upon us, usually because of the position which we hold within its management hierarchy. It carries the backing of the body politic and, as such, can be used to force through a decision. In a modern state, judges, the police and various public servants possess the same sort of legitimate power as Pilate had due to his position as a Roman official. The Jewish authorities needed Pilate to use his legitimate power to get rid of Jesus; they themselves did not possess the necessary power.

Most of the time, the uses made of legitimate power are straight-forward and non–controversial. Those uses include 'rubber-stamping' and actions which can be agreed upon without too much debate. However, the Jesus situation turns up sooner or later on the desk of anyone who possesses this type of power. Pilate must have known quite well what was going on in front of him. The local power groups were trying to push something through the system. It happens all the time and it must have happened to him many times. Having decided that Jesus was innocent, Pilate tried in an ineffectual sort of way to get Jesus off the hook. Faced with this local pressure group, he gave in to blackmail. In one of the most feeble actions by a top local Roman official that one can imagine, he caved in. Despite the fact that he was responsible for Roman justice in that part of the world, he tried to wash his hands of the matter. Given that his status and power was backed by Rome, there was no way in which Pilate could do that.

Pilate was Governor from AD 26 to AD 36. Josephus records that Pilate found it very difficult to govern the Jews. At the end he became obsessed with the idea that the Samaritans were plotting against him. He showed all the signs of total insecurity, and massacred the Samaritans. Such was the uproar and level of complaint to the Emperor that Tiberius recalled Pilate to give an explanation. It seems probable that Pilate did not end his life in Palestine bathed in glory.

A manager is someone to whom the organisation gives legitimate power over and above that possessed by others around him. Most of his actions will be taken with the agreement of his colleagues and will go through easily. But sooner or later a Jesus type situation will arrive on his desk and he will be faced with the make or break decision just as Pilate was.

As a manager, I dealt with groups of people who were very powerful. Because I gave a lot of advice on the best ways of using management development monies, our paths often crossed. It was not unknown for people to visit me to try to channel funds in specific directions and it was right for them to try to influence my advice. It was not right for them to attempt to hog those monies and to ask me to sacrifice less powerful people so that they could have more. Some chose to rattle their sabres and, if their sabre-rattling developed into a real fight over that money, there was no way in which I could wash my hands of the matter and just cave in.

One of the most common examples of times when we must use our power to force justice into a situation occurs when people renege on an agreement. After much argument and debate, a way forward has been fashioned. Everyone has moved just a little way from their own favoured route. Someone who was party to that deal decides that he can get a lot more of his own way by being difficult, sometimes by actively not co-operating, more often by dragging his feet. The advertising manager agrees not to play a launch of a new product in a particular way, then his approach re-emerges in a slightly different form. The research manager agrees that such a version of the product is beyond the company's means, but the new version of the product looks strangely like the old one. At the end of the day, we use our legitimate power to force through the agreed course of action.

The Pilate situation is often seen when people wish to establish, promote and extend their empires in unacceptable ways. The commercial manager can show that some new product would be a very risky venture. A powerful research and development manager is determined to pursue its development and is prepared to do anything in support of his course of action, including sacrificing a very good commercial manager. If we have control over those people, we should be in no doubt that our legitimate power is there to be used.

Whatever level of legitimate power we possess, it has been given to us to use wisely and in pursuit of Godly ends. The use of that power may get difficult but there are no bowls of water around in which we can give our hands a quick rinse. Life is not like that.

## Things to think about

1   What arguments between rival factions are going on around us at present? What legitimate power structure is supposed to settle those arguments?
2   When were we last faced with the pharisee/high priest faction in our own organisation?
3   What legitimate power have we been given? Do we understand its structure and the ways to make it effective?
4   List the occasions on which we have 'washed our hands' of a situation? What should we have done?

## Prayer

Lord Jesus, we remember before you the shameful use of legitimate power by Pilate which delivered you into the hands of your persecutors and brought about your death on the cross. Teach us to understand the legitimate power which has been given to us and help us to exercise that power in your service. When we are faced with difficult decisions, give us the insight to see an acceptable way forward and the strength of purpose to follow that way whatever difficulties stand in our route.

*Amen*

## 25 The Expert

*'And when Jesus saw that he answered wisely, he said to him, "You are not far from the Kingdom of God"'* (Mark 12:34).

If we read chapter 23 of Matthew's Gospel, we can be left in little doubt of just how critical Jesus was of the scribes and pharisees of his day. The pharisees were a very small group of people, some people estimate 6000 at most, who took their Jewish religion exceedingly seriously and no-one could doubt their devotion. They were not liked all that much. Even the Jews recognised seven types of pharisee, only one of which was held in real respect. What was it that brought upon them so much criticism?

Several facets of their behaviour caused Jesus to criticise them heavily, the principle one being their attitude towards the law. In fact, they had become 'experts' at interpreting the law, and it was one of the main occupations of their lives. In the psalms, especially ones like Psalm 119 which is a long meditation on the law, we see a picture of the law which is a source of strength and joy to the people who tried to base their whole life upon it. Like true 'experts', the pharisees had taken that same law and killed it stone dead. Each individual law was worked through in fine detail, almost to the point where you needed a microscope to read the fine print at the bottom of each page. Tithing was a good example. The practice was to attempt to count in all the main crops which a man had and to tithe them accordingly. Many Jews kept a herb garden for cooking and there might be one single plant of rue in it. ('Rue' is a Mediterranean shrub, with a strong aroma and bitter leaves and greenish-yellow flowers.) The pharisees actually wanted to include that one little plant in the crop tithe calculation. The same was true about washing before a meal; the detail they proposed reduced a sensible practice to nonsense.

However, the man in Mark 12:34 appears to have been the seventh type of pharisee, *ie* one who was held in deep respect. He was probably just as much an expert on the Jewish law as any other pharisee but he had learned how to use his knowledge to provide true insights. He knew that his understanding of God's law had to be used sensibly and not pursued as an end in itself.

Over the years, the number of experts in management positions has increased dramatically. Personnel, computing, management services, planning, accounting, marketing, have all been added, each providing expert knowledge. I used to have the habit of turning over the pros and cons of different courses of action in public until I realised that others were hanging onto every syllable I uttered and using my views as pseudo-scientific reasons for doing particular projects. I came to realise that if I said a piece of machinery would not do the job, nobody argued. I was the expert in that field and that was that. If an expert said that the quality of information about a process had to have such and such characteristics, it was funded accordingly or the whole process abandoned as being un-economical. We rely on experts and we put the future of our organisation in their hands. Experts now hold great power.

Looking at the pitfalls which the old experts in Jewish law fell into will not necessarily tell us all the problems which beset us, but they are an interesting collection. The most obvious one is the unnecessary elaboration which these old experts tried to foist on their people. If you had followed all their instructions, a count-down for an Apollo space launch in our time would have looked like a simple procedure compared with the life you would have been leading then. The temptation for an expert to burden others with irrelevant details is enormous. Along the same line of think-ing, there is a temptation to make others follow detailed methods which we would not dream of following ourselves; in other words, to be hypocrites. Another temptation is not to see the wood for the trees. The pharisee in this story had noticed the trees and the wood and knew their relative importance. We must do likewise. For example, it is no good producing brilliant technical solutions if they are economic nonsense.

The really great temptation that faces the expert is to overvalue his/her expertise. Very often, the practice of our particular subject has been part of our lives for many years. We understand it and, quite often, we love it and get a tremendous kick out of using it. It takes a lot of effort and humility to value other people's contributions to the same extent. The danger is that our evaluation of our own expertise can become much too high, and our expertise can start to displace our other concerns completely and can become utterly and exclu-sively central to our lives. Among other things, it may be that Jesus' condemnation of the first six types of pharisee was due to the fact that they had taken the law of God and made from it a god of the law. Our own expertise carries a similar temptation.

## Things to think about

1   Do we understand the structure and the nature of our own expert knowledge? Do we understand its strengths and weaknesses?

2   Think about a recent use of our expert knowledge. Did we make the simplest possible suggestions, or did we ride hobby-horses and make other people's lives complex?
3   How much real power does our expert knowledge give us? Go through some examples of our use of that power. How could we have done a better job?
4   Do we accept that God wants us to use our expert power which he has given us in his service?

## Prayer

Lord Jesus, you have given each of us special gifts with which to serve you. Teach each of us the temptations which surround an expert and make us determined not to misuse our expertise. Make those skills serve others and not make their lives more burdened. Above all, show us when we are giving our expertise too much importance, making it central to our lives and displacing from that centre our concern for others and for yourself.

*Amen*

# 26  Power to Build

*'Then Solomon began to build the house of the Lord in Jerusalem on Mount Moriah'* (2 Chronicles 3:1).

David, Solomon's father, had wanted to build the temple of the Lord very much, but God said 'no'. Solomon was to do it and in the books of Samuel and Chronicles, we read of the great preparations which he made. Capital was made available, labour was organised, all the necessary skills were obtained, a large variety of supplies were secured and detailed plans were made both for the building and for all the things which were to go inside it. The work is described right from cutting the first sod through to taking in the Ark of the Covenant and the Prayer of Dedication. Each sentence shows Solomon's determination not to fail in any small part of the operation and to drive the project through to a conclusion. Solomon had been given the power to do a great work and he used it—he built the temple of the Lord as instructed.

The history of the world is full of accounts of people who take their gifts, their positions of power and influence, and their energy, and put them together to do great things—for example, Florence Nightingale revolutionised nursing and patient care, and people such as William Wilberforce and Nelson Mandela have devoted their lives to the abolition of slavery and apartheid and the emancipation of coloured people in this world. People are given their positions of power and influence so that they may take part in God's creative processes, and they are expected to have something to show for it at the end of the day. In the New Testament one cannot help feeling that the master expected a hundred per cent return on his gifts of one, two and five talents.

We are unlikely to be a great reformer or a giant of industry, *ie* a five talent man. We are very likely to be a one or two talent man whose contribution to society might be small but will make a big difference when used alongside our colleagues. If we are a stock controller, it matters a great deal if that job is not done well. The availability of essential parts might be in our hands. If we administer a hospital, it matters whether patients wait around in endless queues unnecessarily. If we manage research, we have a duty to make it good, relevant research which catches people's imagination and gives a good return to society. We have not been given power just to keep the boat steady and prevent it from being rocked. In so far as God has given power to us, it is on the clear understanding that we do something positive with it in the service of God and of our fellow men. This is always possible, no matter how limited our power may be.

It is possible that we are another Solomon to whom God has given a major task. We should be careful not to avoid God-given responsibilities. Whether we have been given a large or a small task, it is our duty to do that job with humility and to the best of our ability. Every ounce of determination we possess should go into that job, just like Solomon.

## Things to think about

1  Who are the people around us with the biggest job? In what sense was the task given to them by God?
2  What is our most important task? In what sense is that a positive piece of work for God? How can we improve our contribution?
3  In what sense should we be using our power and influence to allow others to work well?
4  What can we do to improve the jobs which our organisation does?

## Prayer

Lord Jesus, in both your life and your death, you did a great work for us and for all mankind. We know that God gave people like

Solomon the power to do great works for him. Whether it be small or great, give us the insight to see the work which we must do and give us the determination and strength to do it.

*Amen*

# 27 Justice : A Basis for the Use of Power

*'You shall not pervert the justice due to your poor in his suit . . . and you shall take no bribe'* (Exodus 23:6,8).

Questioning the relevance of the Old Testament to modern life is a very common pastime. We ought to remember therefore that Jesus said, 'Think not that I have come to abolish the law and the prophets, I have come . . . to fulfil them' (Matthew 5:17). There is a great deal in the Old Testament about how we should conduct our lives which is as relevant today as it ever was. In our own age, our so-called permissive age, it is tempting to water down the hard core of ethical teaching which it contains. We do so at our peril. There are lots of instances in modern business life in which we are asked to make a subtle compromise about our ethical beliefs. Two examples will illustrate the point.

The poor need our concern in all ages. It is not only those who are poor in a monetary sense. What about those who lack their fair ration of power? The old lady whom we are trying to evict from her rather tumbled-down cottage so that we can build a spanking new warehouse is entitled to justice and care, even if the project can be shown to be for the good of the whole community. Are we sure that it is for the good of the whole community and not just our balance sheet? If we start short-changing such people, or setting loose the whole power of our legal department on them—beware. It is not unknown for a rather irritated and frustrated senior manager to say more or less, 'For goodness sake, get her out, at any price and in any way'. But Jesus made it clear that the old lady is entitled to justice and to our concern.

Bribes are probably just about as common in modern society as they ever were. Few people have difficulty in recognising the straightforward variety, and the Bible instructs us to have nothing to do with them. But what about the not-so-straightforward variety: the business lunch, the free trip to an international seminar, the diaries, the bottles of Scotch, the desk sets, and so on? These are the modern business bribes which abound. As a very young computer manager, without very much purchasing power at all I might add, one of the very best and most unexpected meals I had ever seen was given to me by a computer company. In those days, I was very naive. The distinction between a genuine marketing initiative—such as the launch of a new product—and a bribe, can be pretty difficult to draw. Often, there is not an explicit deal associated with the gift to us, just some sort of vague understanding that relationships will be as good in the future as they have been in the past. There is room for concern in all of these situations.

The Old Testament concern for our ethical principles is very broad and very deep. If we take that concern seriously, it is probable that our principles will be tested at least daily. The fact that the New Testament seems to be more about the love of God for man than about ethics should not blind us to the fact that we are also dealing with a righteous and just God. When he tells us that we must live honest lives, love has not lessened that honesty, quite the reverse. Love has transformed it and made it many times more demanding. The old woman in the cottage in the way of our new warehouse is entitled to justice and caring concern, which far outstrips the district valuer's estimated worth of her delapidated old cottage. She is entitled to treatment in line with her status as one of God's children. She is entitled to the concern shown by the Samaritan for the traveller in Jesus' parable.

We will have our eyes opened if we read the Old Testament in order to discover our ethical and social responsibilities. As managers, we need to do that and then to carry out those duties within the limits of power given to us for that purpose.

## Things to think about

1   Suppose we stick to simple things like justice and bribery —have we worked out what our responsibilities are in these fields?
2   What was the last sticky ethical situation in which we found ourselves? If we cannot recall one, is it because our sensitivities have been anaesthetised by our practices?
3   Are we embroiled in any system which is fundamentally unethical? Think carefully.
4   When we are thinking about the allocation of work, even in our own departments, do we respond to bribes, such as the remark which flatters our ego, or do we try to get the best man for the job?

## Prayer

Lord Jesus, teach us that, as well as being a God of love, you are a God of justice and of righteousness. Teach us that love does not change or destroy our need to do what is right in this world and in our work. Give us the strength of mind to do those things which must be done no matter how difficult they are.

*Amen*

# 28 A Bridled Tongue

*'A soft answer turns away wrath, but a harsh word stirs up anger'* (Proverbs 15:1).

One of the main ways in which we exercise power as managers is through our use of words. The Bible is full of warnings against the sinful or the unwise use of speech. In Matthew, Jesus says, 'I tell you, on the day of judgment men will render account for every careless word they utter' (Matthew 12:36). Ecclesiasticus says, 'Who is he that hath not offended with his tongue?' and 'Curst is the whisperer and the double-tongued'. A brief look at a concordance will convince anyone that the list of warnings is huge.

Lord Geoffrey Fisher, Archbishop of Canterbury in the 70s, said, 'Life is strewn with orange peel'. There is little doubt that a large proportion of sin in the world is unintentional, made up of unintentional slips on that orange peel and a large proportion of those slips are slips of the tongue. A manager relies on speech so heavily that he is bound to be making slips all the time, and sometimes the slips will hurt people. More often than we care to admit, they will introduce confusion and misdirection into our statements and directives, and other people will go down wrong paths through our fault. The effects of careless speech are serious and widespread.

It is easy to underestimate the part which speech plays in a manager's life even though we know that we do a lot of talking. Studies have shown that managers prefer very strongly to conduct their business by speech. The same studies have shown that managers change their field of interest at an amazing rate and that they spend comparatively few minutes on each topic. They work fast and they work on a wide range of subjects. In these circumstances, we must be prone to making unwise and ill-considered remarks. For these reasons, the biblical warnings are very relevant to us.

If it is part of a manager's job to react quickly and by word of mouth, then we need to develop some strong and good habits. This verse suggests two of them. When we get an irate customer on the telephone, we had better be ready with the soft answer and it is not only in those types of circumstances that a soft answer comes in useful. It must always be right to be able to keep calm and to think and speak in a gentle way. Equally, when the world is starting to fall about around our ears, the last thing which helps matters is a bout of anger. We may feel like blowing our top when we are faced with some lunatic unwise action by a person who ought to know better, but it is not going to help. A habitual high level of control over our tone of voice and anger is a very useful attribute.

Of course, all this does not mean that we do not say unpleasant things and react with passion when that is justified. Nor does it mean that we are double-tongued, saying pleasant things while we feel like saying very unpleasant ones. A soft answer is a calm answer, not a peace-at-any-price answer. An answer devoid of harsh words may still contain facts of life that the hearer does not wish to know. Managers know that the avoidance of real issues is not a course of action that deserves to be commended.

For all of these practical reasons, a manager does well to heed the Bible's words on the use of speech. But there is another reason that bears consideration as well, and, at first sight, it appears not to be so practical. Our speech is an important part of the image which we project to others. We cannot do much about our other features to make them reflect a concern with good work well done, with the use of kindness and gentleness, and other such qualities. Our words can reflect those concerns. With practice, they can show to others parts of the nature of Godliness. There is no better use of a tongue than that.

## Things to think about

1   What are the characteristics of our manner of speech? What are its weaknesses?
2   When did we last feel like biting off our own tongue? Which of our regular patterns of thinking caused that remark? What amends did we make? What amends should we have made?
3   In what ways do our words reflect the nature of Godliness? How can we show more concern for Godly qualities such as truth, kindness and concern for others?
4   When did we last need to raise unpleasant things with another person? How well did we perform?

## Prayer

Lord Jesus, we know that our tongues are instruments both for good and for ill. Make us sensitive to the ways in which we talk to others. Give us the charity and the wisdom to say things which help those around us. May our words show some of the character-istics of Godliness to others. When we speak unwisely or foolishly, help us to see our mistakes and to make amends for our action.

*Amen*

# 29 Judging Others

*'Be merciful, even as your Father is merciful'* (Luke 6:36).

The actions which we take as managers are based on our judgment. Many of those judgments are about people. We decide what skills they have and how they can be used. We judge whether or not they have delivered the goods in the past and whether there were ex-tenuating circumstances if they did not do so. We decide whether they are lazy or industrious or somewhere in the middle. We decide if they have done well. If we are to be able to plan the work of the department, we have no option but to make those judgments and ones similar to them.

In making such judgments, God would have us act with con-siderable generosity. Jesus was clear on one other thing, namely, that our judgments are never to verge on condemnation. The warning is emphatic: 'Judge not, that ye be not judged' (Matthew 7:1). Long before we get anywhere near that state, God would still have us think and act with mercy. We need to think about that word—mercy.

In the Bible, God's ultimate use of mercy is to wipe out our Godlessness, our sin. In New Testament times debts were written on papyrus using ink which was a mixture of gum, soot and water. A common way of cancelling a debt was to write a large Greek letter *chī* over it. On the other hand, one could take a sponge and eliminate every part of the writing very carefully and the debt vanished. When Paul talks of sin being removed from the record, he is referring to this second method of removing the debt. The mercy and forgiveness of God is such that it is as if the sin had never existed. It is that quality of mercy which we are told to show to other people.

It is really very difficult to find people who are fundamentally malevolent and wish to upset the work of a department, although there are some. On the other hand, it is common to find people who do not understand their role, possess wrong information, do not know how to use that which they have, and so on. The man who puts an injudicious comment in a report, the order clerk who allows the stock of a particular part to run out, or the computer operator who makes a mess of a master file—such people are not malevolent; their fault is probably at worst carelessness. Rather more serious is the man's error when, for example, a store is always left empty, maybe putting the entire plant at risk. The selfishness of that man shows that he puts himself at the centre of his life continuously, and that means that no-one else, including God, gets a look in. The same workman could well be taking all the easy parts of a job leaving his colleagues the nasty parts. That degree of selfishness is verging on malevolence. In all of these situations, a manager must act to correct the trouble, and we are given power for that purpose. Our action is based on our judgment and, whatever the circumstances, those judgments should be generous and merciful.

Mercy is not some academic notion when we come to make these judgments. We are required to give people the benefit of every doubt, to attempt to understand what went wrong, to take corrective action and then to wipe the slate clean. It is only as far as we correct people with their own improvement in mind that we can claim to be acting in line with God's will. But when we get embroiled in major disciplinary action against someone, we should count that a failure, an inevitable one perhaps but still a failure. We are told that the measure which we use when we act will be used in the judgment of our own action. If we want mercy—and we all need it—we must be merciful.

## Things to think about

1  Name a few of the corrective actions we have taken lately. What judgments did we make? Which were generous and which were downright merciless?

2  What are the areas in which our judgments tend to be harsh? Are we justified in being harsh?

3  Which slates have we not wiped clean? Are we still justified in remembering the weaknesses of those people? How can we move towards a clean slate?

4  Are we part of an organisation in which people live with their

mistakes for a long time? Can we help to change that way of working?

## Prayer

Lord Jesus, we thank you that God, in his mercy, sent you to deliver us from our sinfulness and to cause us to grow again. Teach us to understand the weaknesses of others who work for us and to look upon their mistakes with mercy. Teach us that we must always attempt to wipe the slate clean and to start working with them to overcome their inadequacies.

*Amen*

# 30 Blinded by Zeal

*'When Judas, his betrayer, saw that he was condemned, he repented and brought back the thirty pieces of silver to the chief priests and the elders, saying, "I have sinned in betraying innocent blood"'* (Matthew 27:3–4).

The disciples were a band of people drawn from all sections of society, probably just as varied as any other band of 12 which we might find. There were groups inside the 12 such as the fishermen, but we do not know much about how they broke up into sub-groups in the total band. There must have been at least one group who would associate with each other quite closely, namely, the zealots. The zealots must have been rather like the twentieth century freedom fighters in the old colonies, very intense, very nationalistic and prepared to do almost anything for their beliefs. Quite easily, Judas could have been drawn to Jesus by his own vision of how Jesus could rid Israel of the hated Romans. The zealots thought of the Messiah as the one who was going to do that very thing for God's people.

Judas must have been a trusted member of the disciples at one stage; he held the purse. At the last supper, Judas occupied a place of honour next to Jesus. When Jesus gave Judas a special titbit out of the food bowls, that would have been interpreted as a sign of his being honoured. To do that for someone in Jewish society was a particularly friendly act. So what happened to cause Judas to betray Christ? What was he trying to accomplish? If we read the Bible, it is clear that the writers portray Judas as becoming more and more disillusioned with Jesus as time passed. For instance, his unpleasant words about the ointment which he thought was being wasted on Jesus could have been because he thought that the money obtained by selling it could have gone into funds for the zealot cause. Judas, the zealot, must have been torn in pieces by the sight of the power of Jesus, as shown in the miracles, not being used in a messianic way to overcome Rome and to restore the throne of David.

It is at least possible that Judas betrayed Jesus in order to force the hand of Jesus. If Jesus were faced by arrest and trial, then surely he would use his power to establish his Kingdom. We do not know whether all this conjecture is near to the truth, but we do know that Judas repented when he saw the outcome of his action. He ended his life in a desperate frame of mind, desperate enough for him to commit suicide when he saw his life's work as a zealot and as a disciple shattered to pieces and Jesus, an innocent man, hanging on a tree because of his actions.

We all have our causes, and we all have our pet schemes. They are the apple of our eye, the thing about which no amount of reasoning has any effect on us. We know that a particular market must be approached in a certain way; we know that this particular piece of research contains the salvation of the organisation; we know that this particular variety of managerial restructuring is going to release the pent-up potential of the division. And so, we latch onto a boss in the totally irrational firm belief that he is going to deliver the goods for us because he appears to be going in our direction. He may be very much wiser than we are; he might sense that the market is really an illusion; he might see that to bring the research to fruition is beyond our financial strength and would spell disaster; and he might be able to see that our form of restructuring will sow seeds of acrimony which will tear the company to shreds for the next decade. The boss might be first class and want to go in approximately our direction, but he can see the flaws in our proposals and will not follow them.

How do we react to our boss's refusal to adopt our policy? Disillusionment with him and with his performance is a very common reaction. What about going on to try to force his hand? As managers, we are not paid to sit there quietly like lapdogs—we have a responsibility to fulfil. We can argue by forcing his hand, we are doing our job, but we are very unwise if we underestimate the risks which are associated with this type of argument. Our own desperate belief in our ideas can blind us to their consequences, and, if we are wrong, those consequences may be beyond our wildest imagination and spell disaster.

At the end of the day, Judas saw that he had got it all wrong. Despite his repentance, he was shattered, but it was too late; the damage had been done.

## Things to think about

1   What are our pet schemes which we are pursuing at all costs?
2   Who are we counting on to bring them to fruition for us?
3   Have we got some blind spot which might lead us into trying to force someone's hand against his better judgment?
4   Just how far down the road of betrayal are we willing to go in our stubbornness and blindness?

## Prayer

Lord Jesus, teach us not to be blinded by our own beliefs about the future, especially when it is the future of our own ideas. May we respond when wiser people than ourselves show us a better way forward, even when that means that we must abandon our ideas. And when we are following another leader, teach us never to betray his trust in us.

*Amen*

# 31 Compromise

*'Again, the Devil took him [Jesus] to a very high mountain, and showed him all the kingdoms of the world and the glory of them; and he said to him, "All these I will give you, if you will fall down and worship me". Then Jesus said to him, "Begone, Satan! for it is written, 'You shall worship the Lord your God and him only shall you serve'"'* (Matthew 4:8–10).

If there is one thing that every manager knows, it is the meaning of 'compromise'. Finding a way forward among many different courses of action is the very stuff of management. One seeks to get commitment from one's subordinates by taking account of their views, and the result is a compromise: other colleagues have opinions which are not the same as our own, and so we come to a compromise; or orders come down to do something which cannot be done, and so a compromise is sought. It is a comparatively rare event to be able to follow a course of action which is believed to be the best of all possible ways forward.

Some agreements to do things in a different way, even when

everyone feels that they have given up something they hold dear, are good. In so far as each person feels that the final package represents something like the totality of what was best from everyone, then they feel that the process was wholesome and it commands their respect and commitment. It is often the case that coming to an agreement, starting from many distinct starting points, results in a very much better solution being adopted in the long run. That process can be exciting and exhilarating. It is as if one were participating in something much greater than that which would otherwise be possible; an act of real co-operative creativeness. This is when compromise is at its very best.

But there are other sorts of deals which are sordid, and it is foolish to pretend that there is always a way of avoiding getting involved. Often, if we do not get involved, the price of our lily-white hands is a much worse deal for the people who will have to live with the result. A departmental head leaves and is not to be replaced—how are the remnants of his empire to be shared out? It is quite pointless to try to maintain that the deals which will be made are always in the best interests of the organisation. Sometimes they are, but very often one can observe some shady arrangements. If there was any real power vested in the old department, the new deal can degenerate into a fight. When individuals are competing for jobs in a reorganisation, making sure the 'best' man wins can be a tricky business. One's backing for a particular candidate is often tempered by thoughts about what will be acceptable. If two departments are put together into a partnership which neither likes, the compromises involved in choosing king and courtiers can become sordid, but however sordid it may be, we cannot opt out.

Of course, not all bad deals are the result of this type of circumstance. When Jesus faced his temptation to do a deal with the Devil, it was just after his baptism, and that must have been one of the high spots of his life. It is easy to make a throwaway deal in the middle of a sequence of things that are going well. A person's most vulnerable time is peculiar to that person; some are careless when they are excited, others when they are depressed. It is so easy to say, 'Oh, he's a good chap, it will all work out'. 'Know thyself' is good advice, especially if our knowledge teaches us when we are weakest and most likely to make mistakes.

The real deal facing Jesus in the wilderness was rather different from all of these. If he had worshipped the Devil, he would have been exchanging good for bad, mixing them up with each other and, in the end, undermining the whole moral basis of action in this world. Since Jesus must have been the one to tell his disciples of this experience, it is reasonable to think that he was trying to make one important point in each of these episodes telling of his encounter with the Devil. If the folly of mixing good and evil was the message which he wanted to stress, there is no doubt that it is a grave warning about the type of compromise which we should be willing to make. In whatever form they appear, once our compromises start to mix up evil and good, to make actions revolve around bad principles, in other words to substitute the Devil, whatever that means, for the God at the centre of our lives, we are on a very slippery path.

In this story, what did Jesus mean when he talked of the Devil taking him to a high place and tempting him in this way? We do not know for certain, but it is an experience which managers sometimes share. Sometimes we sit back and think about the place in which we work just as if we are looking down on it from a high place. We see its departments, its people, its power structures and, if we are at all ambitious, it is a very tempting scene—oh for a bit more power; oh for a bit more popularity; why not try a few short cuts? Perhaps in the desert, Jesus thought long and hard about the methods by which the Kingdom of God could be established. Given his imagination, he would have been able to see all the tempting short cuts, but he took none of them.

As managers, we are going to have to continue making compromises. The question is, where do we draw the line?

## Things to think about

1   List the compromises we made recently. Which were the good ones and which were the bad ones?
2   Which compromises were we least happy about? Analyse our reasons. What could we have done differently?
3   Is there some set of arguments which are always going on and always resulting in compromise? What can we do about the basic cause?
4   What was the best compromise we made recently? Think about its goodness and its richness.

## Prayer

Lord Jesus, you taught us never to abandon our principles. When we make compromises, keep us mindful of the risks of being unprincipled. If we are forced to make deals which we would rather avoid, help us to lessen the harm which they do and to take steps to talk to, to comfort and to strengthen those who are hurt by them.

*Amen*

# 32 The Abuse of Power

*'But when the tenants saw the son, they said to themselves, "This is the heir; come let us kill him and have his inheritance"'* (Matthew 21:38).

The interpretation of the parables can sometimes be difficult. Because of the context in which it occurs, this particular parable appears to apply to the Jewish nation and its relationship with the Messiah. This may be true but it has a general meaning as well. Like all good masters, having given the tenants a job to do, he gets out of the way while they do it for him. But things go wrong and various people, including the son of the household, are sent to try to get things back onto the right tracks. However, the tenants have acquired a liking for following their own inclinations and abuse their position. In pursuit of their own ends, there were no limits beyond which they would not go. In other words, their power had corrupted them.

Whether this parable was meant to apply specifically to the Jewish nation, we shall never know. Its general message is true in any case. Selfishness combined with sufficient power to permit a man to pursue his selfish ends is an almost fatal combination. Power is given to us to use for a good purpose, and the second we start to abuse it, as these tenants did in the parable, we are on a slippery slope. As our abuse of power starts to be our regular pattern of behaviour, our slide down that slope becomes ever more rapid.

We tend to think of power in fairly grand terms but this parable applies to modest varieties just as well. If we use our positions to channel the good jobs, the perks and the good things of life at work towards our friends and ourselves, it may not be absolutely wrong but it is an abuse of power. If we push the good contracts towards those suppliers who treat us well, that is sailing very close to the wind, even if it is not against the rules or against the company's interests. We can drift from these small beginnings into worse things and not know it simply because our sensitivity and conscience have had the edge removed from them.

One of the deadly things about the abuse of power is that it can become part of the atmosphere. If a director of research starts to view an international conference as a perk and fails to question its relevance to his work adequately, that attitude will become part of the atmosphere of the laboratory. The attitude will sap people's will to concentrate on what is relevant and their research will suffer. Once it becomes accepted that we can use the odd five per cent of our power to feather our own nests, we have ceased to understand that all power belongs to God and is for use only in his service.

Another deadly thing to look for in the abuse of power is when it becomes accepted that people can be manipulated. The Old Testament is much more severe towards those wrongs which are directed against people, than it is when only goods are involved. We do not often find ourselves able to prevent someone receiving their inheritance but we do often have an influence on their rewards. When we start rewarding friends more than our critics, we should think about our actions very carefully. We must be scrupulous in the way we deal with God's children and not abuse our power.

If we have power, we must accept that we shall use it wrongly sometimes. We should start to get worried when we cease to be aware of having used it unwisely. Power does corrupt if we allow a lust for it to get into our blood and we must watch for the smallest tendency to abuse our positions.

## Things to think about

1   List the wrong uses of power which we have encountered lately.
2   Which actions of our own have we been least happy about? Did we have an alternative? Why were we concerned that we had misused our own position?
3   When did we last feel that some person was being ill-used? Could we have done anything about the action or something to comfort that person?
4   What is the structure of power in our workplace and does that structure give particular groups unfair advantages?

## Prayer

Lord Jesus, you showed us the great dangers which surround our use of the power given to us. We know that power can bring great corruption to people when they misuse it. Keep us ever mindful of the need to use power only in those ways which are acceptable to you. Help us to recognise and to shun possible abuses in our own lives.

*Amen*

# 33 Vengeance

*'Repay no one evil for evil, but take thought for what is noble in the sight of all'* (Romans 12:17).

Throughout the Bible, unrepented sin and evil bring retribution, either at the direct hand of God or that of his agent. A whole people, Israel in particular, might be chastised and corrected at the hand of another nation, the Assyrians for example; David might be forgiven for the Bathsheba episode, but he did not avoid all of the consequences of his action; and there were consequences for Judas when he betrayed Jesus. In the Bible, retribution was often severe and very much in line with the seriousness of the sin committed. But there was an important principle behind all such retributive action: it was always the action of the Lord. '"Vengeance is mine, I will repay," says the Lord' (Romans 12:19), and the implication is that we are not to get into the business of avenging ourselves.

As managers, our power to reward shades off into power not to reward and this, in turn, can become corrupted and cause us to visit a person's misdoing upon him, to take vengeance. It is part of our job to take corrective actions and as those actions become more severe, our temptation to get angry with the people concerned becomes greater. When it appears clear that the actions which we are trying to correct are jeopardising some of the best laid and most important plans, our anger is liable to overflow into fury and our actions against those responsible tend to be less controlled. Such are the routes to vengeance.

Undeserved retribution comes in many forms—when our praise lacks generosity, our reward system is suspect; when we respond to an average performance by relative indifference, we should not expect improvement; when we respond to someone's poor performance or his poor relationship with the rest of our organisation with carping criticism and a denial of our responsibility towards that person and his work, then we must expect further deterioration. Each pattern of work and each pattern of reaction from us is moving on a downwards spiral towards the total collapse of a profitable relationship. When we respond to bad work and to total social failure by retributive action, we have failed just as much as the other person, and whatever we call it, we are not a hair's breadth away from vengeance.

The total organisation in which we work is on the same sort of spiral. Some actions are pushing it upwards, others are pushing it downwards. The only way of stopping an organisation slipping downwards is for individuals to put in more than they expect to get out, for every time we take vengeful or near vengeful action, we have pulled the whole organisation downwards. Power to reward, to encourage, to praise and to cause to grow, these we do have and these are actions designed to move people upwards. We have to have power to correct, but we do not have power to avenge ourselves.

## Things to think about

1   List those actions which we have taken in which there has been some element of retribution. Was it justified and, if so, how?
2   What is the structure of disciplinary action in our organisation? How near to being vengeful is it?
3   Have we seen a set of actions which spirals downwards and how do we react to it?
4   Is there any sense in which we feel that someone has got off too lightly and how do we see God dealing with that situation?

## Prayer

Lord Jesus, we remember that we are not to reward evil with evil and that we are to seek what builds up people and makes them noble. Make us ever mindful of the dangers of power, especially the temptation to reek vengeance on another person. If our response to another person is ungenerous or contains any element of vengeance, correct us and comfort and strengthen those whom we have wronged.

*Amen*

# 34 The Handover

*'And the Lord said to Moses, "Behold the days approach when you must die; call Joshua, and present yourselves in the tent of the meeting, that I may commission him"'* (Deuteronomy 31:14).

If there is anything more difficult than exercising power and responsibility, it must be handing that power and responsibility on to someone else.

Even allowing for the effects of later editing and the undoubted tendency for early historians to exaggerate in order to make a point, there must have been a very great man at the centre of the Moses story. His spiritual, religious and national achievements were enormous. Moses must have been a giant of a man, full of drive and determination, very wise and full of insight and, above all, a loyal and devoted servant of his God. After 40 years in the wilderness, the view of the promised land across Jordan from the high hills which he could still climb, must have made his blood race through his veins and every nerve in his body tingle with excitement. Just a few more miles and he would be there—his life's work done. The urge to go those few more miles must have been almost overwhelming, but instead of recording such a triumph, such a climax to his great life, the last few chapters of Deuteronomy describe the way Moses handed over power to his successor.

Joshua had been Moses' right hand man for some time. Joshua was going to have a difficult time with Israel and Moses knew that because he was a realist. Israel was a young nation, prone to all sorts of divisions and very fond of abandoning its God. Moses had to make sure that Joshua was established as a leader, so he started by making a system of his own teaching so that it would be a base on which Joshua could build. He went round all the different tribes, blessed them all, and undoubtedly talked to them about the future. He went through the whole ceremony of handing over—a ceremony that people would remember; only then did he climb Mount Nebo to the top of Pisgah (Deuteronomy 34:1) where he died, and Joshua, his established successor, led the 30 days of official mourning. At his death Moses was given that great title, 'Servant of the Lord', a wonderful description of his past life, and Joshua was now handed a great new job, the occupation of the promised land.

At any time, it is not easy to give people their head and to let them get on with the job. It can be dreadfully difficult to hand over power completely, especially when we are about to retire from the scene completely. Even in their old age, good managers have much to offer, in wisdom if not in energy, and we will feel that we still have a lot to offer when we go. The thought of someone else doing our job in a different way is not altogether palatable, no matter how philosophical we may be. It is very tempting to have a last good fling, to put the finishing touches to a last few schemes even if we cannot really afford them, and to launch that pet project that we have been hankering after for the last 20 years. It is so tempting just to cross over Jordan and set things up for Joshua on the other side.

It is often said that the job of a chief executive is to develop his successor. Even less senior managers are not doing a good job if they remain indispensible and cannot take time away from the job. Eventually, all managers will have to hand over completely to their successors, not just for a little while, but for ever, and just as Moses did that very thing so well, we must make sure that power is handed over in an appropriate way. Perhaps Moses' ritual was a wee bit complex but his basic steps are worth study: tidying up our own work, preparing our followers to change their loyalty and being seen to hand over the reins, are all worthy steps for anyone to take.

Power is something that God gives to us to use for him for a little while. If ever we need to give up some of that power for a time to another person, it should be done constructively and gracefully. And when we come to relinquish it completely, we should hand over that power at least as well as we ourselves have used it.

## Things to think about

1   Think about a power handover that we have seen. What characteristics did it have?
2   Is our likely successor working for us now? What are we doing to prepare him for leadership?
3   When we give people jobs, are we careful about establishing their position and making sure that others look to them for decisions and not to us? Go through some examples.
4   God willing, most of us know when we are going to retire. Have we given serious thought to making ourselves dispensible over our last year at work?

## Prayer

Lord Jesus, we thank you for the great example of Moses' leadership, for his wisdom in preparing Joshua and for his obedience in handing over leadership to him. Teach us never to hang on to the power which you have given to us, to prepare and to allow others to use it on our behalf and, in the end, to hand over wisely the power which you have given to us.

*Amen*

# 35
# A Prayer About Power

Lord Jesus,

You taught us to say, 'Thine is the power';
  help us to realise that the power we have comes from God and is
  to be used in his service.

God has given us different sorts of power;
  help us to understand the true nature and limitations of the
  power given to us.

You have shown us that men can do great things with God's help;
  help us to accept responsibility with humility and to do those
  things which you would have us do.

You have taught us never to abuse the power given to us;
  make us sensitive to the consequences of all our actions.

You have shown us the dangers of compromise;
  keep us alert and upright when we are forced to compromise.

You have taught us to fashion all our actions using truth, wisdom,
  justice and mercy as our guidelines;
  help us to study and understand those gifts and to use them with
  diligence.

At the end, help us to relinquish power with grace and to help to
  pass on to others the means to do God's will for them.

*Amen*

# Part III
# Ethos — The Way Things Are
# Done Around Here

# 36
# Foundations

When people live together for a while, they develop a way of life. If they did not do this, then life in that society would be very difficult. People new to that society may be given a rule book of sorts but, for the most part, they pick up the way of life by being around for a few weeks or months. There are many different words to describe this aspect of any society; 'ethos', 'climate' and 'way of life' are a few of them. Whatever word we use, we are describing something very fundamental about that society which determines many of its other characteristics.

A family circle is probably a society which we all know very well. We can sense and feel what sort of a family we are in within a few hours of being admitted to its circle, and we can feel the relationship which exists between parents and children. Any amount of kindness, gentleness and consideration which exists in that group cannot be disguised for long. The type of life they lead, their value systems, their togetherness, all of these things which go to make up their family way of life show through and determine the things they feel and the things they do. Our own family ethos is probably the one we know best and the one which influences us most.

Workplaces have an ethos as well and many management scientists have carried out research into the ethos or the climate of workplaces. These scientists talk about things like behaviour norms, attitudes towards learning and communications, general management style, the types of pressure and sanctions which are used on people and so on. In a sense these are the foundations on which that society is built. That ethos determines the nature of that society and what it will be able to accomplish.

Jesus was very explicit in his teaching about foundations: a house built on rock stood; one built on sand fell down. As managers, we have a duty to lay down foundations for our society at work which are rock solid. The question, 'What sort of place would God have around here; what sort of ethos would he create?' is important. We need to think about how to lay down foundations in accordance with his plan.

# 37 The Basic Foundation

*'You shall love the Lord your God with all your heart, and with all your soul and with all your mind'* (Matthew 22:37).

This commandment is the basis of Christian life, whether it is lived out at home, at work, or anywhere else. Jesus did not invent this law; it had been at the centre of Judaism for a thousand years. In Deuteronomy, it is recorded how this law was established and how the Jewish people were instructed that they must teach this law to their children, whatever else they did or did not do. Unlike the love which the Jew was to have for his neighbour, his love of God was to have no bounds and was to consume his whole being. It was to be a love which dominated his thoughts, his emotions and his actions, and it is to be so with us also.

What is it that makes it so important to put God unreservedly at the very centre of our lives? We will all find different answers to this question but there is one which applies generally: a firm Christian belief is quite simply that life is very much better when we do this. By putting God at the centre, we get onto a path which leads to real life, a life whose quality is beyond our wildest dreams, a life which has been completely and utterly transformed and translated onto a much higher plain. Throughout the Old and the New Testaments this same message is clear. In Deuteronomy, a reason for obeying the law is said to be, 'He will watch over our nation and keep it prosperous'. In the New Testament, Jesus says, 'I am come that you might have life and have it more abundantly'.

Deciding what it means to love God in this way is the work of a lifetime and there are no slick answers about how to do it. A starting point for getting onto the right path for this work of a lifetime is the thoughtful realisation that, even in earthly terms, love is not some sentimental, easy-to-practise activity. To love God will demand dedication and hard work. If an easy-to-practise activity is not love, our second question must be, 'Are there any foundation stones that we can lay down to start building an understanding of what exactly it is?' Three suggest themselves to me: *first*, if we love someone we like to be in their presence; *second*, we treat things which belong to and are created by a loved one with respect; and *third*, we attempt not to offend loved ones by acting or behaving in ways which displease them.

*First* then, how do we start to practise the presence of God in the workplace? The presence of another person in a room has two effects: on the one hand it constrains us; on the other, it facilitates actions and encourages us to act positively in line with the other person's attitudes. One cannot act in a mean and selfish way in the presence of a person who is generous and self-giving. In the presence of a man whose thinking is positive and whose actions are creative, we are bound to try to act positively. As we come to be more aware of the presence of God in our own offices, our committee rooms and on the shop-floor, we become more and more aware of these influences on our behaviour. We cannot be mean or malicious to the subordinate we are trying to correct if we believe that God is sitting in the chair next to him. We cannot be negative towards a plan, no matter how bad it is, if God is sitting there requiring us to take part in his positive plan for the whole of creation.

I have suggested that the *second* way in which we can see our love for another person at work is by observing our reaction to things which belong to them or which they have made. Clearly, as managers, we have power over and handle in a variety of ways large parts of God's created world. We must be able to defend before God our use of that world and the use of it that we give to others. If we manufacture goods, they should not be shoddy. We must be able to defend the ways we use people. If we provide a service, we should be proud of it. We cannot pretend to love God and at the same time work in his world as if that world and the people in it were of little value.

The *third* way in which we can be more serious about our love of God is to consider more thoughtfully what his reaction to our behaviour will be. We know that one of the fastest ways to destroy a relationship on earth is to be indifferent to the reaction of the other person to our own actions. We are fooling ourselves if we say we love God and yet at the same time set little value on truth, honesty, compassion, love for others and the many other attributes which go to make up Godliness. To love God implies that we strive to be Godly. The odd bit of fiddling at work, an attitude which undervalues colleagues, the lack of a positive approach to work, such basic attitudes do not please God and, if we behave in these sorts of ways, we must change. To love God implies that we are willing to be made just, honest, truthful and all the other things which serving God implies.

We can love God because he first loved us. But we should be in no doubt that a commitment to return that love implies a complete change in our lives; and that change affects work just as much as any other part of life.

## Things to think about

1   If we are in the presence of someone for whom we have a great love and respect, we change our behaviour. If we really believe that God will be sitting next to us in the office tomorrow, what difference will it make?

2   When we were dealing with the material things around us at work yesterday, in what specific ways did our handling fall short of our target?

3   What are we involved with at the moment that falls short of the ethical standards which God sets? What, if anything, can we do about it?

4   Do we consider that the love of God should be the dominant influence which determines the ethos and the climate of the place in which we work? Do we sit down and try to work out what that means?

## Prayer

Lord Jesus, you taught us that we must love God with an unconditional love. Teach us what that love for you means at our place of work. May we feel the presence of God around us in our office and may our behaviour reflect our concern for God's standards. As we work, may our love of God determine the way we use those parts of his world which he has placed in our care.

*Amen*

# 38 Danger — Baals at Work!

*'You shall have no other gods before me'* (Exodus 20:3).

Man is a creature and his ultimate goal must be to relate to his Creator—God. The earthly goals which a man aims towards play an important part in his pursuit of this ultimate goal and add to or detract from his relationship with God. There are no hard and fast rules about how to set goals here on earth which contribute to our relationship with God, *ie* means by which we keep on the track as it were. However, there is one sure way of getting off that track completely: that way is to set up other gods to put at the centre of our lives and to worship them.

The Baals of the Old Testament are separated from us by 3000 years of change in thought patterns. We cannot take seriously the idea of bowing down to some carved idol, and because of our disdain for such idolatry and other crude forms of polytheism, we are in danger of overlooking Israel's great and historic contribution to mankind, namely, her monotheism. The gods which we find in our polytheistic, modern society may not be carved idols but they are gods nevertheless. In so far as man bows down and worships them, he is in trouble.

A man's god is that which he places at the centre of his life, *ie* his ultimate concern. A man may have several gods but he usually bows down lowest to one principal deity, a sort of reincarnation of the Roman household god. The common deities in modern society are possessions, money, a hobby, games, a house, the party, a family and so on. Some of these Baals have their good sides—a house-proud wife only becomes a real menace when her god starts to demand fanatical devotion; a husband's golf god only starts to become dangerous when its worship leads to some variety of family neglect. If the worship is not carried to extremes, maybe some of these modern Baals do not appear to be too dangerous but all of them present one great risk. They all displace the true God and prevent a man from becoming a saint, thus depriving him of the stature which is God's gift to him.

At work, one or two special work gods exist, the main one being work itself. Some work is so intrinsically interesting that a person can become completely engrossed in it to the exclusion of everything else in his life. Research projects are often like this. For some of these people, every other part of life, except his work, dies — his marriage, his social life, everything. As these other parts of his life die, he is left only with his work and its grip over him becomes stronger. The god work reeks havoc in a person's family life as he becomes less and less available to those once closest to him. His god becomes not only his ultimate concern but also his only concern. On retirement—if he gets to that stage—his god leaves him in a hopeless and friendless situation. Work can be a very ruthless god once it has established dominion over its worshipper.

Power is the other god to be found around at work frequently. The Lord's Prayer is quite explicit about power; it belongs to God not to man. That power which we exercise as managers comes from God and we must exercise it on his behalf and for his purposes.

A man is in a very dangerous position when power becomes a thing which he grabs and clutches at and uses for his own purposes. When a man starts to love his god power, he is well on the way to justifying all sorts of actions which are questionable. Corruption certainly lies along that path and, even if a man does not fall to those depths, the love of power will distort a man into an extremely unpleasant shape.

Many minor deities exist at work alongside the major ones. We can develop a pet way of doing something and thus we become fanatically devoted to doing it in that precise way; we have one idea and it becomes our ultimate concern; we latch on to some management theory, and it blinds us to all common sense. If we work hard for something, anything at all, there is a danger that it becomes the only thing we care about. We have created a god for ourselves, but graven image or not, we should have no such gods.

## Things to think about

1   What is the thing which we seek most and care most about at work? Has it become a false god?
2   How devoted are we to our work?
3   What do we think about the power which other people and ourselves wield?
4   What is the thing in our lives which comes nearest to being a false god?

## Prayer

Lord Jesus, you taught us to love the one true God and to have no other gods. Show us the things which we make central to our lives and help us to question our devotion to them. Make us wary of the things which we do at work and the power which we wield as managers so that those things never displace the true God from being the centre of our lives.

*Amen*

# 39  Surrounded by Neighbours

*'You shall love . . . your neighbour as yourself'* (Luke 10:27).

Luke records the story of the Good Samaritan as the answer to a lawyer who was trying to get Jesus to define the word 'neighbour'. We tend to miss the real point of this story because we do not understand how that very strict Jew would feel about a Samaritan. In a Jew's eyes, his own nation was first and foremost God's chosen people. In a very important sense, namely, that God would show himself to the world through that people, he was right. But many Jews saw God's choice of their nation as putting them above other nations; even their Roman masters were regarded as little better than the dust under their feet by most Jews, and the Samaritans were even lower. They were the people who, centuries before, had separated themselves off from the true Jews and had set up their alternative holy places and way of life. To the Jew, the Samaritan was the lowest of the low. As Jesus defined 'neighbour' for this lawyer, the man must have stood there in a complete turmoil of mind. His reaction must have been akin to that of a militant racialist fascist being told to go and love a black civil rights leader.

At a different point in the Gospel, Jesus makes another issue clear—the man who claims to love God and yet does not love his neighbour is a liar. Love of God and the love of a neighbour are the two linked foundation stones of the Gospel.

We must also bear in mind what love means in the New Testament. It is not a sentimental set of concepts, rather the purposeful desire for someone's well-being. Just as our desire for our own well-being knows few bounds, so that which we have for others should have few bounds. Patient, kind, not boastful, not arrogant or rude, not irritable or resentful, these are some of the characteristics of love. It never runs out and it is the greatest power for good in the world—such is love.

If a Samaritan could be the neighbour of an orthodox Jew, then we can guarantee that everyone whom we meet at work could be a neighbour of ours. Everyone at work has the right to that type of neighbourliness which is described in the Gospels and the Epistles. We find it at least possible to contemplate moving towards a real love of those whose company we find congenial. But what about the others, the ones with whom we must work whether we like them or not? Not to put too fine a point on it, what about the man who is a pain in the neck, whatever that means in our particular circumstances? What about the man whom we are fighting with over some issue? As managers, we come into contact with all sorts of people — the pleasant and the thoroughly nasty, the wise and the unbelievably foolish, the idiots who spend their time getting themselves and us into untold troubles, and even the naive simpletons who choose to follow a course of action which spells disaster from the word go. When, in a fully justified fit of extreme anger, we feel like leaving these people to the consequences of their actions, we must remember that Jesus did not behave in that manner. He loved such people so much that he died for them, and for us to do likewise is to love.

Love is not only a characteristic of our personal relationships at work, it must inform and determine our organisational relationships as well. One of the kindest things we do for a worker is to ensure that he has a job worth doing. There is little love in an organisation which arranges itself so that internecine strife is inevitable. Love is absent when company policy demands that 'old has-beens' are treated like horses going to a knacker's yard. Love demands that company policy reflects God's and our own concern for our neighbour, and part of a manager's job is to make company policy do that very thing.

God's command to love our neighbour has got to be one of the foundation stones of any society which we create here on earth. People, God's children, have a right to live in such societies, a right given to them by God. We, as managers, have a duty to provide such a society in their workplace.

## Things to think about

1  Is it far-fetched to regard everyone at work, with whom we come into contact, as our neighbours?
2  What particular part of our relationship with people at work are we developing at the moment? How does love affect the development that we are undertaking?
3  What particular part of our company ethos militates most against the creation of a caring society at work? What are we doing about it?
4  What is our own greatest weakness as far as loving others at work is concerned? What can we do about it?

## Prayer

Lord Jesus, you told us to love all men and to regard them as our neighbours. Teach us how to love and care for those who surround us at work, especially those whom you have given into our care as their managers. Help us to work out realistically and yet imaginatively what it means to love those people in practical terms. When the systems which we operate as managers are not based on a proper care for people, make us sensitive to their inadequacies and give us the willpower and strength to change them.

*Amen*

# 40 The Two Ways

*'The Lord knows the way of the righteous, but the way of the wicked will perish'* (Psalms 1:6).

Throughout the Bible, we are told that the way of life of a man is the thing that matters. Whilst an educated Greek thought that abstract concepts and the ability to have them and manipulate them was what mattered, the Jew thought along very different lines. God's actions and men's actions were the key to understanding the world. The Greek contemplated the abstract nature of love; the Jew worked out what it was to love a man. The Greek gods were collections of abstract concepts; the Jewish God of action led his people from Egypt into God's promised land. To follow the Jewish God is to be a person who is going places and who is well on the way.

Two ways are talked about in the Bible: the way of the righteous and the way of the wicked. The way of the righteous leads to love, joy, peace and all the other gifts which God has planned for man. The way of wickedness is the way by which a man separates himself from God. The fundamental difference is a man's desire to place God and the things of God at the centre of his life, or to put something else there, usually himself. The way of righteousness is a determination to find out what the will of God for ourselves is and to make ourselves obedient to that will.

It is true that this stark choice becomes more complex as we start to fill in the details of that choice. In the process of becoming and living out his way of life, a man stumbles and, sometimes, gets very lost. But the principle set forth in the Bible is very clear—the two ways exist and man should attempt, with God's help, to be righteous.

One of the fascinating changes which has happened in public services and companies in recent years has been the way in which they have started to ask more persistently what sort of business they are trying to run. Objective setting can never have been more popular than it is today. It would be cynical and quite incorrect to suppose that their main concern in this questioning is to make themselves more prosperous, whatever that means. After all, the more prosperous an organisation, the more it seems to be interested in questioning what sort of an outfit it should be. It is not uncommon to find some companies wondering about the responsibilities they have towards the communities of which they are a part, the people whom they employ and the public which they serve. On the other hand, there are companies which do not take such responsibilities seriously, which do sail close to the wind in different sorts of ways and, in some cases, end up in court because of their lack of concern. Two ways exist and, whether positively or by default, an organisation chooses its way of life.

An individual at work has the same sort of choice in front of him. He does not have to do a reasonable day's work and he can skimp on every type of responsibility; there are as many ways of not being a particularly good worker as there are hairs on our heads. We can choose to opt out of our responsibility for the community around us; we do not have to take any interest in the problems of those around us—we have the choice. Once, a colleague who was being treated in a totally unjust way came to me with his story; I had a perfect right to opt out and just be sympathetic and say only, 'That's life'. To make such choices is to deny our concern for a righteous way of life.

Whether we are talking about the nature of the total organisation or the individuals at work, a choice about the basic nature of a way of life is always being made. Those choices are determining the basic climate, culture or ethos of that workplace. If we wish to live and not perish, the Bible is quite clear that we must opt positively for righteousness.

## Things to think about

1    What is the nature of the objectives which our organisation tries to set for its people? Do they add up to a righteous way of life?

2    What actions have we taken recently which affect the sort of place in which we work? In what direction did they move it, towards or away from righteousness?

3    Name occasions in the last week in which either our people or we ourselves made less than adequate compromises. What did these compromises do to our sort of workplace?

4    What are the root causes of some of our less than adequate actions? Have they anything to do with our fundamental way of life?

## Prayer

Lord Jesus, God has taught us that we must choose between two ways of life, righteousness and the way of death. You came to make it possible for us to be righteous. Grant that the very nature of our workplaces and the nature of the actions we take allow us to follow a righteous path. When we have to choose between different courses of actions, keep us by your strength on the righteous way.

*Amen*

# 41 Work is Worship

*'Our fathers worshipped on this mountain; and you say that in Jerusalem is the place where men ought to worship'* (John 4:20).

In most people's minds, worship is something that a band of Christians get together to do in a rather odd-shaped building, often using archaic language, on a Sunday morning. The actual meaning of the word 'worship' is labour or service. In particular, labour becomes more fully worship when it is taken and offered to God. Symbolically, when the lay people take up the bread and wine in a communion service, they are offering their work and the products of that work to God to use as he wills it to be used.

In the Old Testament, there was constant tension between the priests and the prophets about the nature of worship. For the priest, the temple was the only place where man could really come near to the presence of God and so a highly developed worship ritual existed in that place. However, the prophets took a different stance. Zephaniah was clear that the nations would bow down, each in his own place (Zephaniah 2:11); and Malachi believed that nations would worship God in every place (Malachi 1:11). Jesus ignored rather than rejected the priest's concern for ritual, but he supported the prophets. This verse is talking about Mount Gerizim which the Samaritans had substituted for the temple as the place where God could be met. The woman in this story was asking Jesus where she must take her offering, Jerusalem or Mount Gerizim, and Jesus replied at neither, but to offer it anywhere in spirit and in truth (John 4:23).

The general drift of the Old Testament is away from ritualised offerings towards the offerings of a life's work which is worthy of God. Both the psalms and the prophets are almost fanatical in their condemnation of empty ritual. The Lord wanted justice, kindness and concern for others, not a wide variety of empty sacrifices of various types: a man's life work was the true worship. If we follow this theme, how do we turn our modern work into worship? How does that management report or that last batch of goods sent out through the warehouse door on a Friday become true worship, an offering to God.

Whatever else it may be, worship is about praise and thanksgiving, and there is a great deal of room for both of these things in a report and in connection with that last batch of goods and every other job completed. We can thank and praise the people who make our work possible; we can praise and thank God for the achievement; we can introduce joy into the business of thanking and praising people and God. It does make a huge difference when these three things—praise, thanksgiving and joy—are present in a workplace. Work which is seen in this light and which is offered to God in this way has become worship.

One other way of transforming our work into worship is to do it well. There is nothing quite like a piece of high quality work if we want our people to have a deep sense of satisfaction and pleasure. It does not matter whether it is a small thing which took a lot of skill to create or a large building that decorated the town; if it represents good workmanship, people will want to offer that work to others and through them to God—that offering is worship.

There is often a great deal of a man in his work. That is true of an ordinary workman just as much as it is true of a great artist, and as a man offers his work to God in worship, so he offers himself—that is true worship and that must be good.

## Things to think about

1 How much praise, thanksgiving and joy is there in our own workplaces?
2 Think of the last job which was done to a very high standard at work. Did we look on that job as something which should be offered to God in praise and worship?
3 What are the things at work which we produce regularly? Is there any way in which these can be made part of our worship?
4 Are there things at work which we worship unworthily? Money? Power?

## Prayer

Lord Jesus, you taught us to worship you in spirit and in truth in every place. Show us how this can be done at work. Help us to recognise praise, thanksgiving and joy as essential parts of worship and help us to surround others and ourselves with these things at work. May we all offer our work to you daily in praise, with thanksgiving and with joy.

*Amen*

# 42 Joy and Pleasure

*'Thou dost show me the path of life; in thy presence there is fullness of joy, in thy right hand are pleasures for evermore'* (Psalms 16:11).

The psalms have been a source of comfort and strength to men for some 3000 years. One reason for this is their deep realism and the ways in which they talk about problems which touch men's hearts. It is almost invariably true that the psalms talk about troubles in the context of absolute confidence in God and the joy and pleasure which come from being one of God's men. For example, Psalm 13 is all about God forgetting the psalmist, right up to the last two verses when it explodes into a message of trust, joy and victory. Psalm 22 is one of the loveliest of the psalms, about a man forsaken by God, yet, in the second half, it is all about confidence in God. This verse from Psalm 16 is a typical example of the psalmist's great optimism and belief in ultimate victory and joy.

Joy and pleasure in the Bible are not of the skin-deep variety which might be confused with living on some sort of idyllic island paradise in the sun. Joy in the Bible is set against the realism of the cross, fights for justice and struggles to establish the Kingdom here on earth; joy comes out of caring for the needy and the weak—it is based on service for God and our fellow men. Throughout the Bible, that struggle is part of the same pattern which we find in the psalms and it always leads to fulfilment, joy and pleasure which are the things which God wills for his people.

In a very real sense, the same pattern can be seen at work, because no-one achieves anything at work without a struggle. If we try to put in a new computer system, we can guarantee to pass through trials and tribulations before we see the benefits of that system, and, no matter how well intentioned we may be, if we try to introduce a new set of personnel policies, we will be misrepresented in some quarters and run into all sorts of difficulties. More in line with some of the psalms, we may try to award a major contract with scrupulous fairness, only to find ourselves beset by others seeking to push their own interests. As with the psalmist in Psalm

22, we may feel completely removed from the presence of God in some run-down factory out in the sticks where problems have been allowed to fester for years and where the atmosphere is one of distrust and hatred; for one reason or another, God does not appear to be around in these situations.

In what sense is it proper for us to exude a sense of joy, victory and the real pleasure of God in these circumstances? Certainly, there are ways of thinking and acting which are not proper: the naive foolishness which pretends that problems do not exist or that there are easy solutions is not proper; a sense of joy is not the same as misplaced humour designed to chivvy everyone along into a better mood and outlook on life; a faith in God which leads to joy is not the same as some pie-in-the-sky belief that things will turn out alright in the end.

Ultimately this is God's world, and ultimately the cross means that all our battles have been won. The first of these beliefs is our basis for joy and hope in every situation. The way of the cross is our own path to victory, a victory that brings joy and peace. We go to that factory out in the sticks in the sure faith that it is part of God's world, and even in the most run-down place we can start to build on that foundation. So, we build, bit by bit, by hard work, fashioning each stone with which we build before we put it in its place, and we live out the cross by taking the brunt of other people's hate and resentment until we win them over to our vision of victory. We can see and share that sort of hope wherever we look and join the psalmist in his mood of ultimate confidence even in the worst situation—such faith, hope and joy is proper.

## Things to think about

1   List a few of the things at work which have caused us joy and pleasure in the recent past.
2   Think about some of our misconceived attempts to be humorous or over-optimistic in the face of genuine trouble. What should we have done in those circumstances?
3   In general, what should we be doing to enhance the genuine joy in their work of the people who work for us?
4   Think of a situation which has become tiresome and is causing our people to become ill-tempered, lacking in patience and disgruntled. What went wrong? What is the first step that can be taken to get things right?

## Prayer

Lord Jesus, we thank you for the joy and the humour which do so often fill our lives. When we see others sad and despondent, give us concern for them. Teach us to want and to be able to share our joys with those people and with others. When situations have gone wrong show us the first step to take to put them right again and to make others joyful.

*Amen*

# 43 Growth

*'And other seeds fell into good soil and brought forth grain, growing up and increasing and yielding thirtyfold and sixtyfold and a hundredfold'* (Mark 4:8).

The parable of the sower is one of Jesus' best loved stories, but because we spend so much time thinking about the tares, the stones and the thistles, we forget sometimes that it is fundamentally an optimistic story. One of its themes is growth and even the seed which becomes only thirtyfold is a remarkable example of that growth. Many of the Kingdom parables are about growth, movement, change and becoming. Those stories include the one about the seed growing in secret, the one about the mustard seed and many others, all built around the exciting idea of someone bursting into a greater, more abundant and better life. The whole of the Bible is about a God who is leading his people ever forward, and about the growth of Israel leaving oppressive Egypt, and continuing right through to the fullness of the Kingdom of God.

If we accept that growth and becoming are an essential part of the Kingdom, this has important consequences for the sorts of places which our workplaces must be if they are part of the Kingdom: they have got to be places where people grow. For this reason, staff development cannot be regarded as an optional extra which 'progressive' management adopts in line with a somewhat stringent budget. A right to grow comes from God and, as managers, we have a duty to make that happen. What is it about the ethos of a workplace—'the way things are around here'—which makes it a place of growth? Answers vary, but some generalisations seem possible.

*First*, we must believe in the future and we must believe that our unit can be better tomorrow. If we are in public service, then that can be improved; for example our homes for the mentally handi-capped can be better; education can be improved—we can make all these things happen. In industry, the answer to 'What is better?' is more complex, especially in an era of automation and mass unem-ployment. Despite all the difficulties, the fundamental *raison d'être* of the workplace is to create, to become and to serve: that means growth—social growth.

A *second* growth principle is about individual people. As well as being agents of social growth, people themselves grow, and sociologists have suggested many patterns for that growth, some of them concerned specifically with the workplace. Basically, people start by learning, go on to work, accept local responsibility, go on to major responsibility and perhaps, in the process, become wiser. That is a growth process on which we, as managers, have a major influence, and it is our duty to fashion that growth so that our people reach their mature state.

In the New Testament, and in the parables in particular, growth and the Kingdom are inextricably intertwined. The Kingdom is always about people in society, people who are so precious that their very hairs are numbered. The society is always on the move towards godliness and a deeper love of its members for each other, and a workplace must have the same nature and be a becoming society. Those growth processes, processes of becoming, are the same processes which brought Israel out of Egypt and caused the prophets to develop their vision of God; the same growth processes caused the apostles to become saints; the same growth process is going on today and should be happening in our workplaces. What-ever else is true about the Kingdom of God, it is meant to be a growth business.

## Things to think about

1 Is growth one of the things which we see as a gift from God to each of the people who work for us? Take several individuals and test the answer.

2 Take the person in our department who seems to be most often at the end of the road as far as we are concerned. Can we make him grow any more?

3 In what sense is our community at work growing? If the answer is 'Not at all', should we be doing something about it? If so, what?

4 In what way should we be growing?

## Prayer

Lord Jesus, you teach us that life in the Kingdom means growing in stature towards yourself. Teach us to look at every person at work as someone who is growing. Show us the part we must play in that growth and help us to fulfil that role.

*Amen*

# 44 A Manager's Prerequisite

*'And God gave Solomon wisdom'* (1 Kings 4:29).

Alongside the priest and the prophet, a third professional class was recognised in ancient Israel—it consisted of the wise. Proverbs is probably the best known of the books of the Bible called wisdom literature and it was the product of this third professional class. The function of the wise was to fit man into the ordered world which God had created, and their counsel covered all facets of life in society, both those parts related to the individual in that society and those which determined broader aspects of social life. The book of Job is about an individual, while much of Proverbs is about a particular class of person. (For example, there is advice on how to treat widows.) We would think of the wise as being the people who deal with the secular world but we must not forget that our concept of a secular world would seem very strange to a Jew. All the world belonged to God and the concern of the wise was to see that man lived the best and fullest lives in God's world.

The wise had a reputation for being able to say things and to use words in line with an order of things given by God. Some of their sayings were electrifyingly dramatic, such as the famous incident when Solomon discovered the true mother of a child by the judgment which he gave (1 Kings 3:16–28). At other times, their sayings sound just like good secular interpretations of godly principles; for instance, many of them apply to the oppressed, the downtrodden and the weak. Proverbs 23:10 bids the Israelites not to 'enter the fields of the fatherless'. And again, a large section of Proverbs is concerned with bringing up young men in a sensible way. Usually and, unlike the law, the wise worked with particular situations in mind, and in those situations the wise man was trying to find the way forward to a better and more mature society.

There are similarities between the position of a modern manager and the wise in Israel. It does not matter how good a company rule book might be, a manager spends most of his time out on his own trying to find a wise way forward. In Old Testament times, wisdom was transmitted by word of mouth in most cases, and research has shown that, today, word of mouth is the manager's favourite way of giving decisions. Wise sayings enable someone to pick his way through various sorts of minefields, gently but with great persistence, and the story of Job is just such a tale.

Every manager knows how it feels to skate on thin ice, he has been in situations where every pause, never mind the words he utters, counts. If you are counselling someone or sorting out a major problem, an unwise word can spell disaster. Wisdom, the characteristic of Israel's third profession, is as much in demand today as it ever was, and as managers, we use it to shape our future and that of our workplace. When we face situations in which we cannot forecast accurately, we need wisdom to keep our opinions open; when we try to correct someone, we need wisdom if we are to save the situation; often, we need wisdom to sort out warring factions when they come to blows; we need wisdom to set a course which everyone can follow; we need wisdom just about every time we do anything—in fact, as managers, we need wisdom full stop!

Today we think of wisdom in terms of experience and, maybe intelligence, in the loose sense of that word. In the Old Testament, it is clear that the source of wisdom was God—Solomon asked for and obtained his wisdom from God. If we think carefully of the people we know who are wise, it will be plain to us that what they have is more than experience and intelligence; their wisdom is always something akin to a gift. We need that attribute so much that it is almost one of our prerequisites for doing our work well. Perhaps an issue for us is whether, like Solomon, we ought to be prepared to ask God for it?

## Things to think about

1   Do we accept that we need wisdom if we are to do our job? Name some examples of our need for it.
2   What was the last bit of thin ice on which we skated? How skilful in the use of the words were we?
3   In practical terms, do we think of our experience and possibly use of intelligence as the only ways of becoming wiser?
4   Would we be willing to ask God for wisdom in doing our job? If we did, what areas of our activities would we expect to start changing?

## Prayer

Lord Jesus, we thank you for the teaching about wisdom in the Bible and the examples of it which we see around us. We thank you for the experiences in this world and your work within us which have given us such wisdom as we possess. Teach us that the ability to deal sympathetically and wisely with our colleagues is one of your greatest gifts to man and its use is one of our greatest services to others. May we learn to ask for and to use such wisdom in your service.

*Amen*

# 45 A Goal for Our Service

*'Truly, I say to you, as you did it to one of the least of these my brethren, you did it to me'* (Matthew 25:40).

This passage is about the Last Judgment. In it, Jesus says that the people who will be called blessed are those who have served the sick, the strangers and the hungry; in other words, those in need. Although the people who were serving others in this way did not see their Lord in these folk in need, Jesus was emphatic that he himself was being served in a very direct way. Later in Matthew chapter 25, Jesus is equally emphatic that those people who could not see himself in the hungry, the thirsty, the sick, the strangers and the poor, and had not served them, would be condemned at the Last Judgment.

When we walk through the office door in the morning, we do not expect to meet the people on Jesus' list. Although a variety of research reports have told us that the underprivileged do exist in our society in great numbers, most of us still think that our welfare state should deal with the problems. However, all this does not mean that the people whom we do meet in the office do not have problems and needs which are of concern to Jesus, because they *do* have problems, and they have them in abundance. The lonely, the frustrated, the overlooked, the unhappy—they all exist; the list is endless. Each one of these people has a right to be served if we are following Jesus. Do we see our Lord and Master calling us to serve him in each one of them?

It is very likely that a high proportion of the people around us are attempting to deal with a problem. The middle-aged will be attempting to deal with their elderly parents and their rebellious teenagers as well as trying to adjust to a major change in them-selves; sadly, someone is bound to be in the middle of divorce proceedings; the young will be fighting to leave their mark on the world; the old will be anxious about their future as retired people and will be looking back and trying to assess their achievements. The list of problems to be found in a workplace is endless, and it can be argued that a manager has no responsibility in any of these fields and, sometimes, our interest in such fields will be resented. But it is theoretical nonsense to pretend that we can ignore the total person in our attempts to manage their work. We can and we ought to adjust our style so that we serve such people, not make their problems larger unnecessarily.

A manager must be one of the best placed people in modern society as far as having opportunities to serve others go. By his instructions and through his advice to others, he can serve them and put order into their lives in many different ways. We can extend that role by becoming more aware of the desperate needs of others as we do that job. Jesus is saying in this passage that, by meeting the needs of others in this way, we serve him directly and fulfil one of our highest callings.

The people who responded to the needs of others in this passage in the Gospel, were unaware of the significance of their actions. If someone is in need, the best if not the only way to help that person is to give them the whole of our attention and to concentrate totally on that need. If someone comes to us for career guidance, for example, we give that guidance as if it were to Jesus when we grapple as best as we can with the career problem at hand. If men come to us in dispute with each other and are imprisoned by their own prejudices and entrenched positions, we do our service to Jesus when we coax them away from their stalemate into a more meaningful mutual relationship. We do not serve Jesus by ignoring the specific problem or attempting to relate it to some vague religious principle which will probably hinder rather than help. We serve the hungry by giving them food, the prisoners—of whatever sort—by releasing them from their bonds, and we serve our office colleagues by dealing with their situation as well as we are able to.

As managers, we should expect to serve others unstintingly in their own specific ways. That is our way to serve Jesus in them.

## Things to think about

1  In our own organisation, who are the hungry, the thirsty and the prisoners?

2   How can we serve them as their manager or their colleague?
3   If we could see Jesus in each one of them waiting to be served, would it make a difference?

## Prayer

Lord Jesus, teach us to be more aware of and sensitive towards the needs of the people who work around us. Help us to respond to those people as best we can in order to meet those needs. Teach us that such service is the fulfilment of our calling and that through such action, your will can be done and great joy can be released into the world.

*Amen*

# 46  The Modern Scapegoat

*'And when he has made an end of atoning for the holy place and the tent of the meeting and the altar, he shall present the live goat; and Aaron shall lay both his hands upon the head of the live goat, and confess over him all the iniquities of the people of Israel, and all their transgressions, all their sins; and he shall put them up on the head of the goat, and send him away into the wilderness by the hand of a man who is in readiness'* (Leviticus 16:20–21).

'Scapegoat' has changed its meaning over the last 3000 years, but since we are better acquainted with its modern meaning, let us look at that.

If we have been a manager for any length of time, we will know people who have been made to carry more than their fair share of blame when something has gone wrong—scapegoats are fairly common. Our language for describing our scapegoat process is very rich: we can 'pass the buck' or 'find a whipping boy' or 'get out of the line of fire'. The Old Testament phrases in the Leviticus passage catch many of the concepts behind our modern usage. We do confess our sins over our scapegoats and make sure that they carry all our iniquities and transgressions; we do heave a sigh of relief as we 'send them away into the wilderness'; and we certainly do know all about 'having a man who is in readiness' to complete the job efficiently.

Of course, we need an appropriately sized scapegoat to correspond to the size of our modern sin. The contract that goes all wrong, involves long delays and additional payments to the contractor; this needs a really big scapegoat, someone near the top of the tree, at the pinnacle of his career. In the public service, for example if your policy for providing proper resources for an underprivileged group comes unstuck, then you need a big scapegoat: the Director of Social Services will do as a scapegoat for a case of child beating; or a suitable consultant or nurse will do for ill-treating the mentally handicapped in some ancient Victorian institution. Whatever the situation, the principle remains; a big sin needs a big scapegoat.

Of course, it is a fact that, unless they have been blind, deaf and completely incompetent, many other people should have known about the problem and, in many cases, have been told about it by the potential scapegoat. If a large contract has been going out of control for years, any competent board of directors should have known about it. If the programme for rehousing the elderly or the mentally handicapped is not working it is the elected and other members of the authority who should correct it. A wild flurry of activity when some sort of action becomes inescapable followed by the identification of a suitable scapegoat does not atone for the sins of a corporate body or its other senior managers.

Not all scapegoats are large ones, however. Small ones are much more common. Monday morning liverishness can accentuate the manager's need for a scapegoat. If one of our projects is going wrong, probably through our own fault, then a good round-up of all the people involved can do wonders for our guilt feelings. Of course, one of the best minor scapegoats is the one who has just left: the really good chap who has moved on to better things can easily become a scapegoat when he is replaced by someone who is less competent. Fortunately, most minor scapegoats are allowed to return from the wilderness, but the issue for a manager is whether they should be sent there in the first place.

This modern concept of a scapegoat has little to do with the Old Testament. At best, it is a warped and mis-shaped reflection of the original idea. Sin is a fact and the way in which we deal with it in the society in which we live will shape that society in some very fundamental ways. Rooting out things which undermine a society meant to produce work is an important process. Idleness, greed, cheating and lack of consideration for others are some of the sins of a workplace and we usually associate a modern scapegoat with the presence of some such sins as these. These sins must be dealt with and, apart from the gross injustice to the scapegoat, the trouble with our modern scapegoat is that the real sins are usually covered over.

## Things to think about

1 Identify the last major and minor scapegoats in your workplace. Think about the two incidents involved.
2 Did we do anything about the last major scapegoat by identifying some of the corporate responsibilities that were not carried out?
3 What are we doing about our own present crop of minor scapegoats? Pretending that they do not exist?

## Prayer

Lord Jesus, grant that we may never knowingly help to create a modern scapegoat. When we do, grant him your strength and comfort and give us recognition of our failure.

*Amen*

# 47 Caring for the Weak

*'As for the man who is weak in faith, welcome him, but not for disputes over opinions'* (Romans 14:1).

This verse is part of a passage in which Paul is discussing people who, for religious reasons, are considerably distressed when they are asked to eat certain types of food. We are not only centuries away from that sort of situation in time, but our thought forms are totally different from someone in that sort of dilemma. Our minds tend to boggle at the idea that meat that has been offered to some pagan god will harm us. It was the case however in the first century that if you went out for a meal with a non-Christian friend then the food which was offered to you would, in all probability, have been sacrificed at least to the household god. Paul was quite clear in his own mind that such a thing did not matter one iota, but he was also quite clear that, if necessary, such food was to be avoided for the sake of Christians who were not too sure on that issue. And he was clear of another thing too; arguing about such things did not get you anywhere.

In our jobs as managers we have to deal with the weaker members of our teams, those people who are not too sure of their ground. At least two of our common types must bear a striking resemblance to some people with whom Paul had to deal. *First*, there is our own rule-book man, who must have been like some of the first century Jewish converts. In our strength, we might know that our company rule book is there to facilitate good management, not to strangle it with red tape. But our weaker colleague badly needs the strength which a set of rules appears to give him and he might be shocked and bemused by our adoption of what he sees as a cavalier attitude towards the system. *Second*, the young, intelligent convert must have found some basic Christian teaching pretty hard to understand and he must have needed time to work it through. We see plenty of the same young men who should make it through our company system in the end, some with flying colours, but they get lost due to inexperience in their early days. These are only two examples of our weaker members, and many more exist. Paul says that we are to welcome such people and that we are to help with their growth problems.

Paul's other point, the futility of most arguments, is equally relevant to our situation. In a religious context, it is certain that we will never argue a man into the Kingdom of God, simply because it is God himself who draws men in, not us. The example to others of a life spent purposefully and intelligently in service is a much more potent mechanism for teaching others. No amount of discussion will replace a good pattern to follow and we can provide that in our lives. If we want someone to organise things better, show him how to do it; if we want someone to control the use of his time more effectively, show him an example by the way we control our own time. Action and example are worth a million words, even if our discussion with the man is not a dispute. If we get alongside a man and teach him how to work by working with him, then we are learning how to welcome the weak.

Jesus promised his disciples that he would be with them right to the end of the world. He makes his strength available to us and expects us to call upon him. Growing into and with Christ is not a long series of disputations in which he tries to knock some sense into us, rather it is a process in which he gets alongside us in our weakness and welcomes us. If we want to bring out the best in our staff, especially the weaker ones, we must avoid those things which trouble them, avoid long silly arguments and get alongside them instead.

## Things to think about

1  In an understanding frame of mind, go through the weaknesses of your staff. What can you do to help them?
2  Go through the last abortive argument that you had with one of them. What alternative action could you have taken?

3   Pick one of your weak members of staff. If you really did pull out the stops, what could you do to get alongside that person?
4   What is the prevailing attitude towards the weak in our workplace?

## Prayer

Lord Jesus, in our weakness, we thank you for the strength which you give to each one of us. Teach us to take special care of the weak around us. Grant that our actions may never cause them anxiety or seem to them too risky and rather unwise. May we control our speech when we are tempted to argue with them and may we say only those things which will give them strength. Instead of arguing with them, show us how to get alongside them and to work with them.

*Amen*

# 48  Casting Out Fear

*'There is no fear in love, but perfect love casts out fear'* (1 John 4:18).

Management scientists are very interested in people in organisations. Chris Argyris is one such scientist who has spent a lot of time working on the themes of self-realisation and self-actualisation. He suggests that these two factors are affected by the stage to which an individual has developed: the inter-personal skills which exist in his workplace and the nature of the organisation for which he works. He suggests that most managers fail to involve people in their work by the use of appropriate inter-personal skills and that, instead, they resort to various types of autocratic action. They generate a wide range of justifications for that type of action: 'There isn't enough time', 'I'm paid to know the right answer'—the list is almost endless. Whatever the reason, excuse or rationalisation, the result is the same: a management style which drives out commitment and, with it, joy, pleasure and many other things.

It is a short step from autocratic management to management by fear. Up to the early years of this century, men were managed by fear very often, and the threat of being told to 'collect their cards and leave' was a very real one. There are still companies in which fear is a dominant part of the company ethos; for instance, target setting which is totally divorced from problem-solving can become a tyrannical, oppressive instrument of management. The salesman can live in fear of not meeting his quota, and, if he does meet it, a company can become greedy for better and better figures. The naive comparison of output figures from different factories which chooses to ignore genuine differences in their productive capacities and local conditions can become oppressive and harrowing for the poorer performers. Such practices have within them the elements of management by fear.

The more brutal varieties of fear are much less common nowadays than used to be the case. It is now quite difficult to sack a man, but more subtle varieties of fear exist in abundance. The middle-aged manager who is not really up to his younger rivals; he can exist in fear. The misfit whose skills belong to an earlier phase in the company's development; he can live in fear. The man whose ideas are different from his boss, especially when that boss regards the department simply as an instrument to respond to his will and has the personality to make it do so; he can live in fear. When some chief officer has been 'parked on the sidelines' to get him out of the way; he can live in fear. If our own juniors do not feel able to come up to us and tell us that our latest set of ideas are nonsense; they too are living in a type of fear. If our juniors feel that telling us their problems is going to be unhelpful at best, they are possibly living in fear. If we are so insensitive that we cannot see fear around us, then there is probably a great deal of personal uncertainty, anxiety and fear in existence.

Some managers confuse respect, which they feel others ought to have for them, with fear. They themselves fear to appear weak; they fear to appear to be caring and they fear the results of being kind and gentle; they can also confuse weakness and love. It takes considerable skill to allow our juniors to criticise our ideas and yet remain their leader; it takes wisdom and foresight if we are to avoid the need to put our older colleagues 'out to grass' in a demeaning and unpleasant way. If we can see the fears which people have and feel with them, we are not weak, and if we can take those fears and work them through with the people who are petrified by them, we know how to love.

In a very real sense, well-considered love for people can drive out the paralysing and destructive fears which can become a feature of our workplaces.

## Things to think about

1   To what extent do we rely on autocratic, somewhat irrational, actions in our own management style?

2  What fears can we detect in ourselves and in our colleagues around us?

3  What is our own attitude to our appearing to be weak?

4  Name some colleague who is obviously fearful at this time. What can we do about it?

## Prayer

Lord Jesus, you came to teach the meaning of love which drives out fearfulness. Make us aware of and help us to avoid those of our actions which generate uncertainty, anxiety or fear in those around us. Help us to recognise and to help those at work who are anxious and fearful. May your love for men be reflected in our actions and may that love drive out their fears.

*Amen*

# 49 Sharing the Glory

*'Let all the inhabitants of the world stand in awe of him'* (Psalms 33:8).

A manager is called upon to be successful. His performance is often built on a wide knowledge of his organisation, its market, its people and, sometimes, management theory and expertise. Having all of these things might be helpful and some might be essential, but, it is not what he gets paid for. He gets paid for his ability to use these skills; in other words, his ability to perform. If he performs well, a manager acquires a reputation; if he performs very well, and especially if this is done regularly and consistently, he can come close to acquiring glory and he is talked about in terms of awe and wonder.

Most of us need to be successful, at least to some extent, and we feel pity often for those who lack success. Managers are required to be successful, but there is a danger in success, especially when its continuing presence starts to lead to pride and glory. To be in the middle of a group which more or less hangs on our every word and fails to question its wisdom, places a responsibility on us which few can bear. Even when we become respected members of the management staff, we would be wise to discourage people from standing in awe of us and, instead, should encourage them to criticise our ideas.

Apart from our own good, we need to discourage people from giving us too much of the limelight so that others get fair treatment.

It is our job to give others their ration of glory and their reward for work well done. A frequent complaint in many teams from junior members who do the work, is that they take many of the inevitable kicks when things go badly and yet receive little of the glory for a really good piece of work. The boss goes off to the expensive party when the contract is complete, and the grateful client heaps praise and presents on the top man. We need to be sure that a lot of that glory does not just trickle through to our subordinates if they are lucky and if we remember—most of it is theirs by right.

If we make sure that the glory, the praise and the awe which do belong somewhere in this world get distributed more fairly, we have still only dealt partially with the matter. The other part concerns our giving glory to God. If we look at a particularly glorious scene or something spectacular made by man, we feel wonder and awe. We should always be on the lookout for things which deserve our admiration and are wonderful in their own right: many are made at work. A finely-engineered aero-engine has a glory all of its own, and the same is true of a fine bridge or building. In our offices, there will be things which have a fineness of their own and we should draw people's attention to them. However small an opportunity might be to show people something wonderful, we must use it constructively.

To cause people to reflect on how such occasions show the glory of God will give us problems. We would look very odd if we launched into an Old Testament type of speech extolling the glories of his handiwork in the middle of a project meeting just because the work is superb. However, with comparative ease, we can deflect the praise which they might give to us onto the work itself. As far as that work is God's creation, at least that will be a start in the right direction.

## Things to think about

1  When did people last heap glory on ourselves?
2  When did our glorification last prevent others from getting their rightful dues?
3  Think of your last success story. Is there any way in which we could have funnelled any of the praise which surrounded that towards God?

# Prayer

Lord Jesus, thine is the glory. We thank you for our successes in our work and we pray that others never stand in awe of us because of them. Teach us not to monopolise the glory coming from our work but to channel it to others and to yourself.

*Amen*

# 50
# A Prayer for a Way of Life

Lord Jesus,

You teach us to love God;
   may we know that we live in the presence of God at work.

You teach us to have only one God;
   may we see and control those things at work which threaten to
   take over the central position of our lives.

You teach us to love our neighbour;
   may we see our neighbour in each of our colleagues.

You teach us to choose between the two fundamental ways of life;
   may our management actions move us along the way of
   righteousness and not the way of death.

You teach us to worship God;
   may we make men proud of their work and wish to offer it to
   you and to others.

You teach us that God makes men joyful;
   may we manage others so that they get great joy from their work.

You teach us that you want men to grow;
   may we see the gifts which you have given to men and help them
   to use those gifts to the full.

You teach us that wisdom is a gift from God;
   may we possess wisdom to manage well.

The Bible teaches us about scapegoats;
   may we learn to accept responsibility and, if necessary, blame,
   for all that we do and the mistakes which we make.

You teach us to care for the weak;
   may we see the limitations of others and make adequate arrangements for them to overcome their problems.

You teach us that love drives out fear;
>   may we never use any type of fear as an instrument of management.

You teach us to give God and others the glory;
>   may we never seek glory for ourselves.

Teach us to think carefully about the nature of the departments which we create around us. Show us their fundamental inadequacies and those places where their foundations need to be reshaped. Give us wisdom, strength and perseverence to carry out that reshaping.

*Amen*

# Epilogue

Lord Jesus,

Each morning, as I leave the house quietly, remind me that I have not left your world.

Each day, as I start my work, remind me that this is the work which you have given to me to do for you.

Each day, as I plan that work, remind me to make that plan my best and to make it for you.

Each day, as I do my work, remind me to make it my best offering to you.

Each day, when I meet people at work, remind me that they are your children, my brothers and my neighbours.

Each night, when I come home and close the door quietly behind me, make me thankful to have been out and about in your world.

*Amen*

# Further Reading

Charles Elliott, *Praying the Kingdom* (Darton, Longman and Todd, London, 1985)

JPP French and B Raven, *The Basis of Social Power* (Cartwright and Zander, Group Dynamics, Tavistock, 1960)

# Notes

# Notes

# Notes

# Notes

# Notes